ALIEN SCRIPTURES

EXTRATERRESTRIALS IN THE HOLY BIBLE

REV. MICHAEL J. S. CARTER

ALIEN SCRIPTURES
EXTRATERRESTRIALS IN THE HOLY BIBLE

3rd Edition

Alien Scriptures: Extraterrestrials in the Holy Bible
Categories:
1. Body, Mind & Spirit 2. UFOs & Extraterrestrials

Printed in the United States

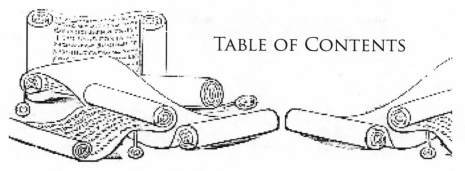

TABLE OF CONTENTS

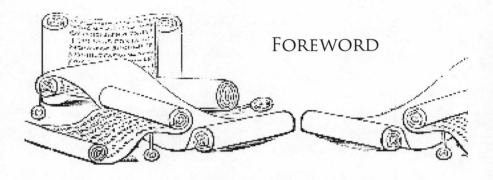

FOREWORD

If UFOs were involved in developing—stimulating—the biblical religion as is suggested in this book, then many questions follow. One is: Is a miracle still a miracle if it is caused by advanced technology rather than by the 'supernatural,' whatever theology means by that? If aliens in other worlds come from a high tech culture, and if they have directed our culture biologically (genetically engineered us), and inspired our religion, then who, or what, is God?

Rev. Barry Downing, author, UFOs and the Bible

Rev. Michael Carter has done a great service for spirituality and science with Alien Scriptures, enlightening the debate on how long extraterrestrials may have been involved in human history. UFOs are not only a modern era sensation, but an ancient one, and Rev. Carter does full justice to the controversial but intriguing subject. His thoughtful examination of what happens at the crossroads of ufology and theology greatly expands the dialog on close encounters for the 21st century.

Harold Egelin , Founder/Director of S.P.A.C.E.

I t has been quite a journey since I first began this work. It started as my Masters of Divinity Thesis for Union Theological Seminary in New York City. Though I graduated twelve years ago, I still recall the acute anxiety I felt wondering if the subject matter would prove acceptable to my Thesis Committee.

Union was, and still is, one of the top seminaries in the country with an emphasis on the "social gospel"—how we might collectively create the "Kingdom of God" here on earth, a kingdom of love, justice, mercy, and forgiveness. Union Seminary has long been known for its rigorous academic standards and also for its commitment to social justice and equality. Imagine me telling my professors that I wanted to write about the Judeo-Christian religion possibly being originated by beings from outer space!

Well, the feedback I received was nothing short of phenomenal. As the old adage goes, "you could have knocked me over with a feather." Not only was I encouraged to write the thesis but my Professor of Systematic Theology suggested that I pursue Doctorate Studies upon graduating. Who knew?

Now I must admit that this was before I added my personal contact experience to the book, and believe me, I was scared to death to even mention it. Without the encouragement of my initial publisher (now retired), Barbara DeBolt at Blue Star Productions, who insisted that I write about my personal experiences, my story would never have been told.

I have seen many changes in the consciousness of the American public since I first began writing about UFOs and The Bible. The Rev. Dr. Barry Downing's book, *The Bible and Flying Saucers,* written thirty-five years ago, in 1968, really opened my eyes and prompted me to read the Bible from a different perspective, a perspective that married the ideas of science and religion. Yet more to the point, Dr, Downing was a clergyperson just like me. Up to that point in my studies, I knew of no minister or priest who would even consider engaging in a conversation regarding the possibility that the *angels* (from the Greek word *angelos,* meaning "messengers") could very well have been extraterrestrial beings, and that these beings made appearances in the so-called Old (First) Testament, the New (Second) Testament, and in the Koran.

That was then and this is now. Times do change; we have TV shows like *Ancient Aliens* where these ideas and others regarding humanity's possible extraterrestrial origins are now routinely discussed. More evangelical writers like Timothy J. Daly, Chuck Missler, Mark Eastman, and Patrick Cook weigh in with their writings our ETs. However, their acknowledgement of ET-life focuses on a more sinister religious agenda, often interpreting "end time" scenarios from the Bible. This interpretation of ETs is not new, and it continues to be pervasive. The new hit show *Falling Skies* on NBC has our visitors being hell bent on taking over our blue/green planet and killing us off and/or enslaving humanity.

Although I do not agree with these writers about the agenda of extraterrestrial life, I do realize that it is so very human to demonize and marginalize those who are perceived as "the other," especially when we do not understand them and we allow ourselves to be ruled by fear. Xenophobia is alive and well on planet earth regardless of whether one is a so-called human being or an Extraterrestrial Biological Entity.

Yet I cannot help but muse on the fact that the three monotheistic religions of history—at least to my mind—were started by beings from another world, beings who some mistakenly thought were gods. In order to continue the exploration of the *three* religions of the book, I have added an extra chapter on UFO's in Islam.

To the question of whether the three monotheistic religions were started by beings from another world, I can tell you that after my close encounters, I can certainly understand why our ancestors might think so. Personally, I know that it took a while for me to heal my own shattered reality after such contact.

You will discover as you read further that I am not suggesting that there is no Creator, just that we might consider broadening our understanding of Creator, that a different sense of Creator might not be the traditional sense of the word. I will leave that up to you, the reader, to decide. The only word of caution I offer is that any concept that human beings create to describe the Ultimate

Reality will forever fall short. We create our gods in our own image; for this reason, the finite will never fully comprehend, much less sufficiently describe, the infinite. If you find anyone who says that they can, I suggest that you run like you know what in the opposite direction.

I can only hope that as you read further you will be open to other possibilities, be open to other questions, and be able to live with the questions for awhile. I wrote this book not to convince you but to engage you. However, I must confess that I do have one agenda in writing this book: I want us to look at the monotheistic religions with fresh eyes for our 21st century world.

This will require in the words of the poet Rumi:

"That our task is not to seek for love, but merely to seek and find the barriers within ourselves that we have built against it."

Rev. Michael J. S. Carter, M.Div.
Asheville, North Carolina
August 29, 2012

To learn more about Rev. Carter's other works and television appearances visit http://www.MichaelJSCarter.com

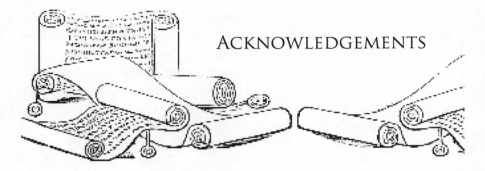

ACKNOWLEDGEMENTS

It would be impossible to list all of those individuals who have nurtured me during this journey of spiritual and intellectual growth. I humbly offer this partial list of those who have supported me through my fantastic and sometimes confusing experiences.

I am forever grateful to Gene Ashley for his encouragement to welcome the visitors and the gifts they brought into my life; to Harold Egelin, Jr. and his support group S.P.A.C.E. for helping me maintain my sanity; and to Dr. Jean Mundy for her love and guidance in assisting me to heal my shattered reality. Thank you Michael O'Brien for your insights and patience, and a special thank you to Bud Hopkins for your skill and compassion. Many thanks to Dr. Barry Downing for your courage in linking the UFO phenomenon and the Judeo-Christian scriptures in your groundbreaking book UFOs and the Bible; thank you, Barry!

Landi Mellas, thank you for making this happen. May God bless your maverick soul.

I am grateful to Union Theological Seminary and especially to Dr. Dolores Williams for encouraging me to explore further the study of possible extraterrestrial contact in the Judeo-Christian Scriptures. Thanks for not laughing me off the campus.

To mom and dad, William and Rosetta Carter, who allowed me to find my way through this whole experience without ridicule, I extend to you a wealth of love and gratitude that causes my heart to overflow. Thank God for you both; I am forever grateful to the Creator for blessing me with you as parents in this lifetime. Kevin Carter, whatever dimension you find yourself traveling in, go in peace; I will always love you. Harold Wise, I love you. I also extend a heartfelt thank you to Sandy Clark for all that you mean to me; thank you for teaching me how to love unconditionally. To my wife, the Rev. Judith Long, thank you for being the wonderful soul you are and for loving me (all these many lifetimes) when I seem not to know how to love myself; what a gift you are to me. Last but certainly not least, I offer my unfathomable love to our daughter Kevyn Mary, who has chosen us to be her parents and students for our time here on planet Earth. Judy and Kevyn, this is always.

In love dedication to Octogon and Tandü.

Thank you for your cosmic love, humor, guidance, and companionship.

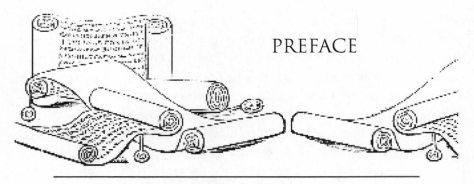

PREFACE

"In the beginning was the word..."
John 1:1

I n the beginning was the word, and these words are a testimony from me, Michael J. S. Carter, about my *positive and enlightening* contact and experiences with extraterrestrial life and how these experiences have transformed not only my worldview, but my life. These experiences continue to resonate in my life and have made me, at least in my humble opinion, a better human being.

I was born on planet earth at 4:09 am in the city of Baltimore, Maryland, on July 9, 1957. My parents were hard working people of color who wanted my brother and I to have an easier time of it then they had, when they were growing up during the Great Depression. They did not want us to suffer the slings and arrows of outrageous fortune that life could bring. In this way they are like most parents wanting a better life for their children.

Like many African-Americans (actually I am of African, Cherokee, Creek, and European lineage) born in this country whose ancestor's are from the southern region of the United States, my parents were and are deeply religious people. They self-identify as Christian. My parents believe in a just, righteous, and at times angry "god." Such a belief system is how we historically, as people of color, survived in a strange and hostile land. Many, but not all, African Americans and Native Americans adapted the Eurocentric model of Christianity and "flipped" it if you will, to resonate with our experience of being the property of other human beings. We sang the song of "The Lord" in a strange and hostile land. Native Americans were also slaves in North America. The Christianity of the privileged and the Christianity of the marginalized and oppressed are two different religions. They cannot be otherwise. For my family, the teachings of Jesus were simply a way of life. Jesus was the example of what it meant to live a committed life, a life of integrity and of authenticity.

Yet despite my parents' best intentions and efforts, I did encounter the slights, indignities, and outright racism of the dominant culture, but I was taught—at home and in church—that things would eventually level out. There was a certain moral high ground that we, collectively as people of color, possessed by letting these challenges roll off our backs, so to speak. The gospel message was that the first would be last and the last would be first. This is not a message that the elites of the dominant culture want to hear. I attended church regularly with no real prodding from my parents. My parents seemed to be delighted that I took such an interest in the church without any pressure from them.

This interest and enthusiasm that I had for religion and philosophy would serve as a backdrop for my contact experiences, as I am one of those people who are not so much interested in the "nuts and bolts" of the UFO phenomenon. That is to say that I am not so much interested in propulsion systems and the like. I do not really have an interest in what makes the ET spacecraft maneuver through time and space (which I assume they do). I am more interested in how the contact experience influences the inner life of the contactee. (Notice that I did not use the word, *abductee*. I was contacted.) My interest lies in how these contact experiences influence the inner life of the individual. In other words, what are the spiritual influences or transformations that occur in the experiencer after he or she has had the visit, and how does this transformation affect their lives as human beings on planet earth?

Growing up, I did enjoy the church services I attended and took the teachings very seriously. With hindsight now, I am sure that I also wanted to please my parents (as any child would) and so that was also a motivation for my attending services on Sunday mornings. The teachings of Jesus from the New Testament did give me a sense of inner peace as well as providing me with a model as to how to live my life. I immersed myself into the life of the congregation by singing in the choir, serving as a deacon, and even serving as an acolyte in the Lutheran Church on occasion, as well as attending confirmation classes. I can still recite the Apostle's Creed.

My parents were Baptists, and I pretty much stayed within the African American church experience and eventually was baptized as a Baptist on Easter Sunday morning in April 1980 at Trinity Baptist Church in Baltimore, Maryland. Prior to that however, I attended various church denominations, such as Lutheran, Pentecostal, and at times Catholic services. Actually, I attended the Catholic services in my teen years because my girlfriend at the time was Catholic and attended as well.

I can recall many times when I would awaken in the morning with blood on my pillow. Not knowing what it was, I thought perhaps my ears were bleeding during the night. Only later did I realize that my nose was bleeding. I thought nothing of it, except that it was rather strange. I can also recall seeing little orbs of light in my room at all hours of the day and night. These orbs were different colors—red, blue, green, orange—and to my child's mind looked like donuts floating in the air. It was like there was a depth to the atmosphere around me and I could see things in 3-D. No one else seemed to notice this but me. At other times I noticed that there were marks, bruises, and scratches on me when I woke up in the morning, but I never really thought about how they came to be there. I rationalized that perhaps I had bumped into something and did not remember doing so. In addition to these anomalies, ever since I can remember, I have always had the ability to perceive various colors around people's bodies and around inanimate objects. Later on in life, I realized that I was perceiving the human aura or energy field, but as a child and youth I did not have the knowledge or the vocabulary to express those ideas.

In my early twenties, I was bitten by the theatre bug and moved from Baltimore to New York City. I had achieved some success and received some favorable reviews while performing in the community theater circuit in the Baltimore-Washington area, and I decided it was time to try my hand at "the big time" in New York City, the theater capital of the world. It was an exciting time—not only living life at an accelerated pace—but a time of intense learning about myself and life in general. After moving to New York, I tried putting new wine into old wineskins, but it would not work. I tried attending a Baptist church in my neighborhood, but I just could not listen to the sermons about sin and saviors and the like. I eventually stopped attending church altogether, because it felt to me that everything I had been taught was a form of brainwashing. At this time I was gradually drifting away from the Christianity of my youth and wrestling with what I truly believed about the cosmos and my place in it. One of my big "issues" with religious doctrine in the West was that the answers are given you before you even ask the questions. Not to mention the fact that some questions are not even tolerated. So the theatre became a way of focusing my creative energies, and I thoroughly enjoyed the craft of acting. I sang and danced in Off-Broadway musicals, as well as appearing in various commercials and films. In short, to quote the late Andy Warhol, I had my "fifteen minutes of fame."

Time moved on, as it is known to do, and I eventually I found that I had little-to-no tolerance for the orthodox Christianity of my youth. I was angry with the Christianity that I was raised with. I have always been a voracious reader, even while attending elementary and junior high school in Baltimore. (In fourth grade, I was reading at a seventh grade level; at least that is what my teacher told my parents at a PTA meeting.) I began delving into books on philosophy, history, archaeology, and metaphysics. I began reading other so-called "lost books of the Bible" and researching scriptures from other cultures. I immersed myself totally into the life of the mind and exploration of the world and our place within it. The more I read the more I began to question church doctrine and wonder what it really meant to be a religious person, a spiritual being. My studies and life experiences made me wonder what kind of "god" would condemn to hell other people who did not believe the same thing as so-called Christians. I also met people from various backgrounds who were not "Christian" in the traditional sense (some were not Christian at all), and yet they would treat others better than some folk I knew who attended church every Sunday. These experiences, as well as my reading and studying, "opened me up." I began to realize Socrates was correct: the unexamined life was truly not worth living. In hindsight, I believe that these experiences also provided me with the opportunity to stretch emotionally, as well to prepare me for being visited by beings from another star culture. Yet no amount of reading could truly prepare me for what was about to happen!

When my contact experiences consciously began for me on December 28, 1989, I resisted any form of organized religion as I attempted to process my experiences and what they meant to me—both with regard to religion in general and to my personal spirituality. I became heavily involved in the study of metaphysics and New Thought philosophies as a result of my contacts with ET beings. Eventually my religious and spiritual questioning and exploration called to me deeply, especially after my contact experiences. I attended an Interfaith Seminary to continue my studies on comparative religions and further my reflections about living a spirit-filled life. After graduation, I was ordained an Interfaith Minister. Later, I would attend Union Theological Seminary and receive a Masters of Divinity Degree. For a few years I was on the path to being fellowshipped as a Unitarian Universalist minister but eventually decided against that affiliation. As I incorporated my contact experiences into my life, my personal theology and spiritual perspective became a blend of metaphysical, Jesus-centered, and Native American teachings. During this time, I have also begun to explore my own Cherokee and Creek roots. At this point on my journey my personal theology is not so much Jesus-centered as it is that I view him as my Brother and one of many beings who have come with a message of love and authenticity for all of humankind. It has been quite a personal and spiritual journey.

"There are more things in heaven and earth Horatio that are dreamt of in your philosophy." William Shakespeare, Act 1 Scene 5 of Hamlet

---

On December 28, 1989, I had a visitation from an extraterrestrial being. Prior to this visitation, I had no interest in science fiction movies or science fiction novels. As a matter of fact, I distinctly recall a conversation I had with a friend while walking along the streets of downtown Baltimore. I don't recall how the subject came up, but he asked me if I believed there was life on other planets. I told him that I did not believe in life on other planets, because the subject was not mentioned in the Bible. More then twenty-five years later my answer seems so ignorant in hindsight. Can you imagine? That was my reply at the time because that was what I was taught consciously or unconsciously by society.[1] Remember what I stated before—that in traditional Christianity the answers are given to us about how the world works before we have even asked the questions. The gatekeepers of Western culture determine what reality for the rest of us is. If an experience or situation does not fit into "the box," it is simply denied. Those who persist in believing in what happens to them outside of this "box" are ridiculed, condemned; and if need be, removed. This is especially true, but certainly not limited to, inquiries about politics, science, art, archeology, religion, and other questions of faith.

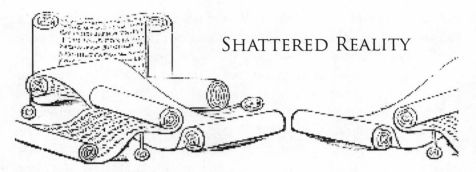

SHATTERED REALITY

My girlfriend (who would later become my first wife) and I had just returned from a vacation in Cancun, Mexico, where we went for a little rest and relaxation and to spend some time on the beach. While vacationing in Cancun, we had taken a day trip to see the Mayan step pyramids at Tolem and Chichen Itcha on the Yucatan Peninsula. The trip was captivating because we learned about the Mayan civilization and their fascination with time as well as astronomy: To this day the Mayan calendar is considered the most accurate calendar known to humankind. We returned home to New York on the evening of December the 27th. The next day was pretty uneventful, and we were just glad to be home. During the early part of the evening of the 28th, I got together with some friends to socialize and to talk about our vacation. I left the gathering around 10 pm to catch the subway home.

Not only was I fatigued, but my body wasn't yet acclimated to the cold weather in New York after the warmth of ten days in Mexico. My girlfriend and I went to bed around 11:30 pm, and I was so grateful to get home to my warm bed. Later, I remember just having to open my eyes and get up for some reason; I don't recall exactly why. I distinctly remember not wanting to get up, because I was warm and comfortable under the blankets. It has always been that if I wake up during the night and open my eyes it is very difficult to get back to sleep. But there was this persistent feeling that I must open my eyes and get up. Suddenly, despite my resistance, I was wide-awake. What I saw was beyond my comprehension. It really frightened me! My room was lit up with a bluish white light—lit up as if it was daytime. Standing at the end of the bed staring at me was a being with an egg-shaped head and wrap-around eyes (I have heard a fellow experiencer describe them a "Ray Band" eyes like the sunglasses that were popular during the 80's). This being was just staring at me, and it truly freaked me out. I don't believe I have ever been that frightened in all of my life.

He (it could have been female but I "felt" it was a male being) was dressed in a tight-fitting silver jumpsuit with a tunic collar, it stood there staring at me. At that moment I did what any self-respecting male would do—I pulled the covers over my head and hoped it would go away! As I did this, I heard a whooooshing sound in my ears as if I were in a windstorm. The temperature changed drastically as if I had left the room and was outside for a moment. I forced myself to pull down the covers from my head to see where I was - and where *he* was. I was lying in bed, but the being was no longer there. The room was dark and all was eerily quite. My partner had not even stirred! I attempted to wake her, but she wouldn't wake up. I could see that she was still breathing, but it seemed really bizarre she would not awaken.

Eventually I went back to sleep. When she awoke for the day, I told her about my experience of the previous night. Fortunately she took it all in stride. Looking back now, that really doesn't surprise me; she was, and is, an extremely open and spiritual woman. She never doubted me, and we were later married, which was to prove to be a tremendous support during the years ahead. Her attitude and support also contradicts the data that shows that many contactees have trouble in their relationships, especially if their significant other has not had the experience.

As for me, I was a wreck. From that night on, I would not sleep with the lights out. I was afraid of what would happen if *he* came again. Here I was a grown man, but I would wait until I was just on the verge of sleep and then I would get up and turn off the lights. When my partner was home, I felt a bit more at ease because I was not alone. Yet she could not help me when the being returned, because she was fast asleep.

I needed to know just what, in fact, had happened. I needed to be able to talk to someone. I found myself wondering if perhaps there were others who had the same experiences and could resonate with my story. I confided my contact experience to a friend of mine who always seemed to be a guide in my life who would listen and not judge; she seemed to have the uncanny ability to come up with advice that proved to be sound in the long run.

My friend was a professional astrologer. When I told her of my experience, she advised that I travel to a neighborhood known as Alphabet City in the East Village in New York. The neighborhood is called "alphabet city" because the streets are named after consecutive letters in the alphabet.

She told me that when I got to a certain street to look at a particular mural that had been painted and to see if the pictures reminded me of anything. This proved important, as I still was not quite sure of what I saw. There was a part of me that did not want this to be some type of ET being from elsewhere. I wanted a more rational explanation. But, I took her advice one afternoon and visited this particular neighborhood and sure enough someone had painted a mural with pictures of gray aliens!!! Those images looked exactly like the being I had seen in my bedroom that evening in December. I was relieved, but now I also feared for my sanity. I did not know what to do.

However, the visits continued for about six months or so, always on the full and new moon. Each visit was frightening to me even though the beings never harmed me. It was *my fear* that was the block to really experiencing the visits and being able to deal with, instead of react to, my visitors. Fear keeps one from being in relationship with the world and with ourselves. As I said before, there was no harm done to me. If anything, my worldview started to change, and I was beginning to see a connection with all of life and creation. My views about what people call "God" and religion definitely shifted to a more inclusive view of Creation. I became more comfortable with the mystery of life and creation and not having to know the answers. At times, I found that the questions were more important than the answers. I also became less wedded to the Eurocentric view of time or history as being a linear experience. I began to really see the cyclical aspects of history and to notice that life and events did not subscribe to any notions we may have of history being simply a straight historical sequence of time.

During this time in our relationship, my girlfriend (and future wife) Sandy worked club dates in the evenings, as a nightclub singer and dancer. She would usually leave around 9 pm and return any time between 1 and 3 am. These club dates were usually on Friday evenings, but occasionally they would be during the week. If it was a new or full moon, I could count on a visit. If Sandy was away at work, I would leave the lights on until the last possible second when I felt I was ready to fall asleep and then I would get out of bed to turn them off. As time went on and because a pattern had formed, I was getting somewhat used to the visits. My fear, while still intense, did diminish a bit. And just as I was getting used to the visits, they slacked off. That is to say that the twice a month visits became less frequent. Sometimes months would go by in between visits, and this began to disturb me. I found myself longing for them to come, and yet I was afraid at the same time. During this time, I slept on my stomach and would not sleep on my back because I did not want to awaken and see them around my bed and have a heart attack from the fear. This may not make sense to you, dear reader, but it made sense to me at the time.

The visits usually consisted of me lying in bed attempting to sleep. The room would become eerily quite, and it seemed that even street noises would cease. The very air became still. At times, it seemed that I would faintly hear a low humming sound in my ears seconds before their arrival. Suddenly and without warning, I would be paralyzed; I could not move or even open my eyes. Instead, they would show me pictures in my head of them being in the room. The pictures were like small icons on a computer being shown in my head. One being would hold out his hand and a ray would come out and touch me, and I would feel like electricity was going through my whole body. On one visit, I did happen to be lying on my back, and I was wearing a rose quartz as this stone has a calming affect on me. When the being sent the ray out into me, the rose quartz I was wearing actually cracked without hurting me at all. Later, I saw that the stone was cracked but not broken. Unfortunately, I later misplaced the crystal. I do not believe this stone was cracked purposely to damage my property, but the crystal just happened to be in the way when the ray was shot towards me. I was paralyzed and could not readily open my eyes during these visits, but I found that if I focused my concentration, I could force them open. When I did successfully open my eyes, the room would be empty. One must remember that I was *wide awake during this visits!*

I felt that I clearly needed to speak to someone professional and soon the opportunity presented itself. Albert Einstein was once quoted as saying "God does not play dice." That is to say that there are really no coincidences in the Cosmos. As I mentioned, I am a voracious reader and always have been. When these experiences began, I read everything I could on the subject. The very first book I read on the subject was entitled, *Encounters* by Edith Fiore, Ph.D. However, the synchronicity of how I found this book was so profound that even Ray Charles could see this was no coincidence. One late afternoon, I was browsing in a bookstore called "The Open Center" located in the SoHo neighborhood of lower Manhattan. As I was glancing at the shelves, I noticed several books on the subject of UFOs. I looked around to see if anyone was paying attention to me and the fact that I was looking at books in this section because I was feeling extremely embarrassed. I feared (that word again) that someone might think that I was crazy. After I assured myself that I was "safe," I picked up several books and Dr. Fiore's was one of them. While glancing through the book, I noticed that in the back, she had a list "symptoms" if you will, of what to look for if an individual suspects he or she is having an encounter with an extraterrestrial intelligence. The book also had a list of professional therapists who specialized in clients who were contactees! I felt that I had hit the jackpot, but there was more to come.

Sheepishly I walked over to the cashier to pay for the books. I felt like a teenager buying condoms for the first time. I could not even look the cashier in the face; I just wanted to pay for the books and get out of there before anyone noticed what I was buying. As he added up the total, he asked me without cracking a smile, "Is this for real or is this just a hobby for you?" When I glanced up, he was looking at the book I was purchasing. He held the *Encounters* book in his hand. I started to lie; I wanted to say, "Of course not man. This is something I am just dabbling in. You know I read this crazy stuff from time to time, but the book is not even for me. It is a gift for a really weird friend of mine. You know how it is." Instead, I answered, "It's for real." What he said next was an answer to my unspoken prayers: "I know a place where you can go and be with others like you. It's a support group. If you are interested I can give you a number to call. I used to go myself." He gave me the number and I called.

When I called, they asked me a series of questions before giving me any information. The questions were a kind of screening, I guess, to make sure people coming to the group were not too much on the fringes. Imagine that—other folks more on the fringe than people who say they had contact with ETs. I thought, "go figure" and took the information they provided. Because the "*Encounters*" book also had a list of therapists who specialized, if you will, in dealing with people who had contact with UFOs and their occupants, I closed my eyes and picked a therapist who used hypnotic regression as a modality to disclose what had happened to me. Her name was Dr. Jean Mundy. She has now crossed over into the spirit world. Yet during our time together, Dr. Mundy used hypnosis to affirm my experience and assisted me in coming to grips with what had happened to me.

"The time will come when our posterity will wonder at our ignorance of things so plain."
Seneca

"In the future the so called Dark-Ages will perhaps be lengthened to include our own."
G.C. Litchtenberg

"When ignorance gets started, it knows no bounds."
Will Rodgers

The support group—SPACE (Search Project for Aspects of Close Encounters)—turned out to be a godsend. The group was formed in March 1992 by Mr. Harold Walter Egeln. Mr. Egeln is an *experiencer* himself, as well as a journalist, and is very well-versed in the phenomena of UFOs and Extraterrestrials.[2] I was welcomed with open arms, and the people I met were open about their experiences. Some had even gone public with their encounters. I was definitely not ready for that at the time, and I admired their courage. In fact, the writing of this book is my first time publicly discussing these experiences. In the group, there were not only others who had the same and/or similar experiences as me, there were also other people of color (though not very many) who were experiencers as well. This was significant for me as it can seem from the literature that ET's only visit people who are European or European American. Naturally, our media perpetuates this image, rarely, if ever, interviewing folk of color who have contact.

Over time, I noticed that although there was varied interest among the individuals in the group concerning the phenomenon itself, most people viewed their encounters as spiritually transformative and positive in their lives. Certainly, there were those in the group who were more interested in the so-called "nuts and bolts" of the phenomena; that is to say, they were fascinated by the propulsion systems of the craft and so forth. Others were more interested in what the government knew or did not know— what could be labeled "conspiracy theories." (I must admit I too gravitate towards this subject as well.) Yet overall, the energy of the group was one in which most people welcomed the experience in their lives despite the ridicule they sometimes endured. Most of the group said the Visitors had transformed them spiritually and now claimed their identities as "Cosmic Citizens," if you will. Barriers such as nationality, religion, ethnicity, race, etc. played second fiddle to the identity of being one with all of Creation. This was important to me because I later became aware that different support groups had different personalities or identities.

I have attended different support group meetings, for instance, where the majority of the experiencers identified as "abductees" and felt victimized and violated during and after their experiences. There are those who feel that nothing of any positive significance came from their visits. While I respect those individuals who have been traumatized and I would never attempt to take that reality from them because the trauma they experienced is valid and real for them, my experiences were different. I feel that my spiritual growth was somehow accelerated and that *in spite of the initial fear it engendered, this was a powerful and positive experience FOR ME!!!!* My opinion and my experiences are not those that receive the most publicity, however. It seems that our culture's fascination with this phenomenon caters more towards the sensational and so-called negative aspects of the visits. Fear, like sex, sells big time in this culture, and thus those are the stories that get the airplay in the media.

SPACE also had a newsletter. This gave me the opportunity to begin my exploration of the potential impact that Visitors in biblical times on the monotheistic religions of the world. As an ordained minister, my interest in UFOs and their occupants tends to focus more on the religious or spiritual dimension to their visits.

The group was just what I needed at the time because the visits continued just not as frequent. I noticed that during the first two or three years of these visits, they would tend to come more frequently and in clusters during summer time. It was during the summer of 1990 that I had my only visit from a reptilian being. On this particular summer evening I was lying in bed awake on my back staring at the ceiling. My partner was again out because she had to work a club date. My ritual of turning out the lights just before I was about to drift off continued, and when I returned to the bed after turning off the light, I rested on my stomach. Suddenly, I felt a weight on my back as if someone or something was sitting on it. I could hardly breathe! I was paralyzed and could not open my eyes. I was terrified, and I tried to calm myself by telling myself that it was just them visiting again. While paralyzed with this weight on my back, I was mentally shown a picture of a being that I can only describe as Spiderman-looking, except that this being was green and scale-y with yellowish cat-like eyes. I heard a voice whisper in my ear, saying, "you're going to be rich and famous" (this has yet to happen by the way). I forced myself up by sheer will and forced open my eyes. To my astonishment, I watched this being simply walk through my window and outside of the building. I lived on the 15th floor at the time! A few nights later, I had a dream in which a being that looked like a giant alligator and walked on two feet was speaking to me, though I never made out what it was saying. These new visitors heightened my fear because I had just barely become accustomed to visits by the so-called "Grays." Just for the record and according to multiple sources, there are many species of "Grays," and yet we speak of them as if they are a monolithic entity.

Before going further, there is something else I must else about my experiences. Perhaps it is because I am a person of color in the dominant Eurocentric culture of these United States, but the mere sight of these beings is both awe inspiring and frightening. They are clearly not from this neighborhood. Yet, I am sensitive to the fact, and I try to remain objective in the realization, that just because a being does not look like me, that does not mean they intend to harm me. I am also aware that objectivity is merely subjectivity under restraint. I mention this because I cannot tell you how many books and articles I have read which indict the so-called "Grays" or "Reptilians" as sinister or evil, while embracing the blond blue-eyed "Swedes" or "Pleiadians" as benevolent and loving. These portrayals may or may not be true. Intergalactic racism is a very real phenomenon in my humble opinion and needs to be called out when it is evident. After all, we humans can be pretty xenophobic when it comes to the so-called "other."

I have written that my experiences have accelerated my spiritual growth and have been very positive in my life. Allow me to be more specific. I have had asthma since I was six months old. I was a sickly child and was hospitalized on numerous occasions due to asthma. I did manage to play sports as an adolescent and even played on the junior varsity football team in high school as a starter on both offence and defense. But there were times when I thought I would leave this world because of the severity of some of my asthma attacks.

A few weeks after my first known contact in December of 1989, this is what happened to me. I was having problems breathing fairly consistently at that time, and a friend of mine suggested that I see a healer. The healer practiced something called "Reiki."[3] I started feeling stronger after the first session, and after going once a week for six weeks, I really felt better. The practitioner encouraged me to learn this healing technique, but I refused. Yet within about two months of my first contact, I began studying Reiki. That contact changed my life and awakened my realization that I am a healer and that this is what I came here to Mother Earth to do. My visitations actually strengthened the Reiki energy I was using. I have given energy to other Reiki healers who have told me that what they receive from me is something a bit more than just the "usual" Reiki energy. When I worked as a hospital chaplain in New York on an oncology unit, I often used Reiki with my patients. For me, it is also interesting to note that after spending so much time in hospitals as a child, I worked as a chaplain for over ten years in hospital settings to assist others who are in need of healing. I happen to be extremely comfortable in hospitals because of my having asthma as a child. The circle is complete.

Let me be clear. There is a difference between being healed and being cured. I have witnessed some miraculous events by using this energy, but I do not diagnose and I am not a doctor. I do not promise anything. One can be cured and revisit the hospital or illness again, and one can die and still feel as if healing has taken place simply by feeling whole and connected to all that is, and thus be ready to make the journey to life after life. As for me, the asthma is not completely gone but now I rarely need my medication to treat it.

To bring this Preface about my journey to an end, I eventually began to lecture about my belief that the Bible is a book about UFO experiences. Now I must say that the Bible is not just a book about UFO experiences, and I am very aware that the biblical stories and teachings give much spiritual comfort to many people. Yet for me, many biblical stories confirm the visits by ET intelligences to this planet. Because of my personal experiences and my research, I am so committed to this belief that I even wrote my Master's thesis on the subject of UFOs and the Bible.

Life never ceases to amaze me. In my 20s, I believed I was moving to New York to become an actor, and I actually found myself beginning a ministry. Certainly, the skills I learned as an actor came in handy when I lecture on the subject of UFOs and the Bible. I have appeared on cable television, published articles in UFO magazines here and in Europe, and appeared on national radio speaking about the subject. I was even regressed by Bud Hopkins after we both spoke on our respective research at a lecture in Hicksville, NY.

For me, it has truly been a journey. These are my experiences. They have been powerful and empowering. My prayer is that this story may be helpful to those on their trail in this life. I hope that I have been of service.

"The only true Alien planet is Earth."
J.G. Ballard

"Two possibilities exist. Either we are alone in the Universe or we are not. Both are equally terrifying."
Arthur C. Clarke, author of 2001: A Space Odyssey

"We are no longer at the top of the cosmic pecking order."
Brian O'Leary, former NASA employee

"My kingdom is not of this world."
Jesus of Nazareth

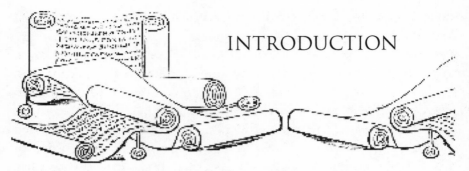

INTRODUCTION

Consider the following facts: two-thirds of Americans say they think there are other forms of intelligent life in the universe; 48% say they believe that UFOs have visited the earth in some form over the years; 45% believe that aliens have monitored life on earth; 37% believe that humans have already interacted with extraterrestrial life forms; 25% believe that abductions have taken place; and roughly 70% of Americans think that the government does not tell us everything it knows about extraterrestrial life forms and UFOs. Additionally, "most Americans appear comfortable with and even excited about the thought of the discovery of extraterrestrial life. Three-quarters of the public claim they are at least somewhat psychologically prepared for the discovery of extraterrestrial life, and nearly half are very prepared. Further, the discovery of or disclosure about extraterrestrial life "would not be difficult for most Americans to reconcile with their religious beliefs. Should the government make an announcement about the discovery of extraterrestrial life, only a very small proportion expects it to change their religious beliefs at all."[4] The Governor of Nevada in April of 1996 officially renamed State Route 375 "The Extraterrestrial Highway" because of the many UFO sightings reported there. The American Astronomical Society has announced the discovery in deep space of a building block for amino acids, the foundation of life on earth.[5]

Unbelievable! Hardly. This information was taken from a 2002 Roper Poll conducted for the SciFi Channel for use in their Emmy Award-winning mini-series *Taken*. That's not all. The Fox Television Network has aired footage of an alleged alien autopsy several times in the past.[6] The conclusions as to the authenticity of the autopsy tapes were left up to the discretion of the viewers themselves. Yet many high ranking government officials, as well as UFO researchers gave their personal perspectives on this fascinating subject.

In August of 1996, scientists studied a meteorite that fell to earth from Mars and landed in Antarctica. They found that the meteorite contained minerals and organic compounds that are evidence of primitive life on Mars. These scientists are speculating that this life may have existed there billions of years ago.[7] And in February 2005, NASA scientists reported that "they have found strong evidence that life may exist today on

Mars, hidden away in caves and sustained by pockets of water. . . (they reported) methane signatures and other signs of possible biological activity remarkably similar to those recently discovered in caves here on Earth."[8] UFOs and alien life are definitely in the consciousness of our culture in the 21st century. The past several decades have seen veritable explosion of movies and television series exploring our contact with extraterrestrial life forms. A partial list includes: *The X-Files, Roswell, Independence Day, The 4400, Taken, Dark Skies,* not to mention Hollywood remakes of *The War of the Worlds* and *The Day The Earth Stood Still.* This is only a partial list. Most of these shows portray the ETs as evil and even horrific to look upon; human evolution is slow indeed. Documentary explorations of the phenomenon include *The Real 4400, Abduction Diaries,* and *Ancient Aliens.*[9]

The March 2000 issue of *Life Magazine* pictures actors from the television show *Roswell.* On the cover are the words, "*UFOs: Why Do We Believe?*" The feature article, written by Cynthia Fox, reports that there were 2,416 sightings of UFOs in 1999 alone, and that one percent of the US population has admitted to encountering a being from another planet.[10] *Life* discovered these opinions in an exclusive poll by Yankelovich Partners, and the results are truly amazing. More men (59%) than women (49%) believe that there is intelligent life elsewhere, and almost half believe the government is keeping information from the public regarding UFOs.

I propose that the Bible is a book of UFO stories. Some may construe this statement as blasphemy or heresy; however, it is clear to me that UFOs or "Unidentified Flying Objects" can be found in the Bible, if one reads with an open mind. To be clear, the Bible is *much more* than just a book of UFO stories, but UFOs definitely figure into the scenario. If my hypothesis is correct, than those beings in the Bible that we know as "angels," might be more appropriately referred to as "extraterrestrials" or "ancient astronauts." They are not to be confused with our concept of a "God" or a "Creator." These beings are intelligent and are most likely brought into being at the will of the one infinite Creator. Having said this, however, this theory does put the traditional Judeo-Christian view of "God" at risk.

This book will explore the fact that this UFO reality is and was fully capable of having brought about the Biblical religion. That is to say that whatever the UFO reality is, it has the power to control our minds and our physical reality so totally that it could have performed every miracle in the Bible. To some, UFOs may carry the angels of God who act on behalf of God. To these individuals, the traditional Judeo-Christian view of God is validated by belief in UFOs, not contradicted by such a belief. However, one could propose the theory that the Biblical religion might have originated with beings from other worlds for reasons of their own, reasons that have nothing to do with "God." Exploring this theory is risky to say the least, for it calls into question the entire basis of the Judeo-Christian religious tradition. It is this risk that makes some religious persons extremely nervous. These risks will be unpacked later in this writing.

This book will specifically explore UFOs in the Judeo-Christian religion, and more specifically the Old and New Testaments. As we begin this exploration, I feel it important to reveal that I am an ordained minister, and I do approach the scriptures with reverence. My purpose for writing this book is to reveal another dimension to the reading of the Bible, a dimension that will stress the similarities between UFO activity in the Bible and UFO sightings today all over the world. This material need not undermine the faith of a believer. At the outset, I want it to be clear that these ideas are my personal opinion and will probably lead to more questions than answers. I am merely asking questions about new possibilities.

Part One of this book will address contemporary UFO encounters, as well as UFO sightings in antiquity. This will include the origin of the term "flying saucer," as well as the infamous Roswell crash in New

Mexico and the possibility of a United States Government cover-up. A brief discussion of other sacred texts and UFO activity will include a look at the Mayan *Popol Vuh* as well as the Hindu *Mahabaratta*.

Part Two will begin our exploration of UFOs in the Bible, starting with some of the evidence of UFO activity in the Exodus story specifically. It will also explore the possibility that Extraterrestrials (ETs) and their crafts interacted with certain Old Testament prophets. I will examine the identity of the god Yahweh from the viewpoint that Yahweh may be from another world or planet. Part Two concludes with my hypothesis that the words "alien" or "extraterrestrial" might be more accurate terms to describe what are more commonly referred to as "angels" or "messengers" in the Bible.

Part Three will address the life of Jesus and his contact with visitors from other worlds and how this might have influenced his ministry. I will look at the stories about the Star of Bethlehem and the Transfiguration in detail. Part Three will also deal with the liberal and conservative Christian perspectives on these phenomena. Finally, Part Four will explore what all of this means for Christianity and its doctrines; if my hypothesis is true and beings from another world created the biblical religion, what will it mean for us today? In light of this hypothesis, how should we look at UFO encounters in modern times?

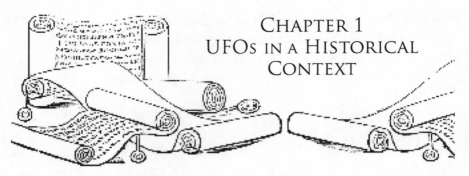

CHAPTER 1
UFOs IN A HISTORICAL CONTEXT

The term "flying saucers" was coined by the press in 1947 following pilot Kenneth Arnold's famous sighting of nine disked shaped objects over the Cascade Mountains in Washington State on June 24th.[11] Arnold was a businessman from Boise, Idaho. While flying his private plane, Arnold witnessed nine flat, shiny objects flying in formation near Mount Rainier, and he compared their peculiar motion to a saucer skipping over water. A newsman inspired by the description coined the term "flying saucers," and this term became a household word as waves of reports came in of strange objects seen in the skies.

Reports came from many qualified observers, such as military and civilian pilots, air traffic controllers, and others whose jobs depended upon their ability to identify objects in the sky. Needless to say, the authorities and the public were alarmed. The FBI and the US military investigated Arnold's sighting. An FBI agent's comments on the reliability of the report are worth quoting:

> It is the personal opinion of the interviewer that [Arnold] actually saw what he states he saw in the attached report. It is also the opinion of the interviewer that [Arnold] would have much more to lose than gain and would have to be very strongly convinced that he actually saw something before he would report such an incident and open himself up for the ridicule that would accompany such a report.[12]

Consider this list of some of the reported sightings of UFOs in the modern era. The list is by no means exhaustive but demonstrates that something is going on in our skies.

July 10, 1952: A National Airlines plane over Quantico, Virginia, observed a light at 2,000 feet which the crew stated was too slow to be a big meteor and too fast to be a lighted balloon.[13]

July 12, 1952: Former Air Force Pilot Jack Green in Delphi, Indiana, was one of many who witnessed a blue-white saucer shaped object high in the sky.[14]

July 19, 1952: At 11:40 pm, dual radar stations at Washington National airport picked up seven objects east and south of Andrews Air Force Base. Andrews also picked up the objects on their radar. Conventional aircraft was ruled out because one object was clocked at 7,200 miles per hour. Some of the objects flew over restricted air space such as the White House and the Capital building. Headlines in the papers the next morning read: "Interceptors Chase Flying Saucers Over Washington."[15]

November 9, 1974: In 1990, the television program *Unsolved Mysteries* carried a story about the experiences of Dorothy Isaat who lived outside Vancouver, British Columbia, Canada. Isaat saw a large UFO in the sky and has photographs that she took of the object.

November 29, 1989: At 5:24 pm, two police officers were on patrol near Eupan in eastern Belgium. There they saw at close range a large, triangular-shaped aircraft with bright lights, one at each corner, and a large red-orange pulsating light in the center of the craft. This object and another like it were observed for approximately three hours as they glided over various areas near Eupan.[16]

March 13, 1997: Flying objects traveled across a large portion of southern Arizona. Witnessed by thousands, videotaped by many, evoking comment from the military and the government, this was the most significant UFO event in decades. The event was much-reported by press and gained worldwide attention. The National UFO Center, in Seattle, Washington, received its first call at 8:16 pm; the Center's director, Peter Davenport, stated, "The incident over Arizona was the most dramatic I've seen... what we have here is the real thing. *They* are here."[17]

These are just a few examples of the thousands of sightings reported in modern times, but the "mother of all sightings" occurred in a small town in New Mexico in 1947.

ROSWELL

On July 2, 1947, a bright disk-shaped object was seen over Roswell, New Mexico. The following day, a widely scattered wreckage was discovered about seventy-five miles northwest of Roswell by a local range manager William Brazel, along with his son and daughter. The authorities were alerted, and the government sent troops to the area to secure the wreckage, including Major Jesse Marcel, a staff intelligence officer with the 509th Intelligence Group, and the debris was taken by plane to Wright Field (now Wright–Patterson Air Force Base).[18]

The United States Army high command made an official statement to the press that a flying object had been recovered and reports were broadcast across the nation. Strangely enough, a few days after the first reports, the military recanted, changing its previous statement to the press: there had been no craft that had crash-landed in the desert. *It was simply a high-tech secret weather balloon.* After the military changed its story, several witnesses came forward to testify that the wreckage was from a UFO and that extraterrestrial (ET) bodies were recovered at the crash site as well. These witnesses also said that they were threatened by the US military and ordered to not tell anyone what they had seen because it posed a threat to national security.

Interestingly enough, in 1997, the 50th anniversary of the Roswell incident, the US government changed the story yet again: there was no weather balloon this time; instead there were mannequins or dummies parachuting from the sky for some type of classified military exercise. Specific details regarding this exercise were never disclosed. Obviously the question remains, why does the story keep changing? Does the US government believe that we are "dummies"? Why does the government maintain top-secret files for something that we are told never happened and does not exist?

GOVERNMENT COVER-UP

Does the US government know more than they are telling their citizens? The following astonishing statement in 1955, by General Douglas MacArthur lends weight to the possibility of the US government being privy to much more information regarding UFOs than it is willing to admit. Douglas had this to say on America waging war in the future:

"The nations of the world will have to unite, for the next war will be an interplanetary war. The nations of earth must someday make a common front against an attack by people from other planets."[19]

Statements from credible witnesses attest to the reality of UFOs. Former astronaut and Air Force pilot Gordon Cooper revealed in a statement to the United Nations on November 27, 1978 that he had encountered UFOs over Germany in 1951. Gordon added: "Several days in a row, we sighted groups of metallic, saucer-shaped vehicles at great altitudes over the base and we tried to get close to them, but they were able to change direction faster than our fighters. I do believe that UFOs exist and that they truly unexplained ones are from some other technically advanced civilization."[20] Certainly, the pilots could be wrong. Human beings are subject to make mistakes in judgment and mental errors. Many sightings can be explained rationally. Pilots and astronauts are not infallible, but their responsibility and position place them in the highest category of witness reliability. Further, pilots and astronauts have absolutely nothing to gain from filing a UFO report. On the contrary, they have much to lose.

In light of such credible witness testimony by members of their own military, the US government continues to vehemently deny the existence of UFOs. Why does the government cover-up the testimony and evidence? The fact remains that there are many reasons for a US government cover-up. One of them could be that UFOs are human-made by one of the superpowers, and that the potential of these craft as weapons demands a high degree of secrecy. That theory is dubious because of the enormous technological feats that are witnessed by these craft. It is simply too difficult to imagine that they are human-made. No doubt the governments of the world would love to capture a crashed disk and back-engineer it to discover just what makes these machines defy the known laws of gravity and do what they do. Another possible reason for the cover-up is that the nations of the world do not want to admit to their citizens that they cannot defend their airspace (as evidenced by the 1952 sightings over the White House and Capital). Such an admission would no doubt prove embarrassing to the government and terrifying to the citizens.

Yet there must be some explanation as to why these sightings frequently occur over military installations. The sightings have increased dramatically since the United States first tested an atomic device in the New Mexico desert in the 1940's. Why were the crafts in Roswell in the first place? In 1949, Professor George E. Valley, a consulting member of the Air Force Advisory Board, had this to say regarding sightings of UFOs:

> If there is an extraterrestrial civilization which can make such objects as reported than it is most probable that its development is far in advance of ours... Such a civilization might observe that on earth we now have atomic bombs and are fast-developing rockets. In view of the past history of mankind, they should be alarmed. We should, therefore, expect at this time above all to behold such visitations.[21]

Some ufologists have speculated along with Professor Valley that perhaps this nuclear testing alerted other extraterrestrial intelligence that a warlike planet could be potentially dangerous if it could reach the frontiers of space. Perhaps we pose a danger not only to ourselves, but other intelligent life forms in the universe because of our tendency to solve our problems violently.

To be sure, there are numerous possible reasons for the cover-up, but the basic motivation behind these reasons is fear. Fear of public reaction by the US and other governments of the world. Fear of what might happen if the peoples of the earth thought of themselves and one another as cosmic citizens as opposed to the nationalistic worldview that is so pervasive in so many nations of the globe. Fear of what would happen if xenophobia, homophobia, racism, sexism, militarism, patriarchy (just to name a few), and all other so-call "isms" were tossed aside even for a moment to acknowledge that we are part of a universal intelligence beyond our wildest dreams. Fear of the far-reaching social, religious, and political effects once the truth is known. Certainly, our earth-based religions (especially the monotheistic religions) would have to rethink the present cosmology regarding who and what God really is, not to mention the age-old questions regarding the universe, how it works, and our place in it. In 1969, reflecting the possibility of an emerging UFO cosmology and theology, the Russian philologist V. Zitsev announced to the world, "Christ was a newcomer from space, a representative from a higher civilization."[22]

It is mind-boggling to me that orthodox Christianity relies upon the 2,000 years-old writings of a group of individuals, concerning a story about a Jewish Rabbi who was crucified by Rome for high treason and allegedly rose from the dead, but cannot believe the modern phenomena of multiple witness sightings (by credible individuals like astronauts and military and civilian pilots) not to mention video evidence regarding the existence of UFOs. Though we have modern evidence, this is not a modern phenomenon; UFOs have been visiting earth for centuries. Before we turn our full attention to UFOs in the Bible, let us now explore what individuals have been witnessing for centuries.

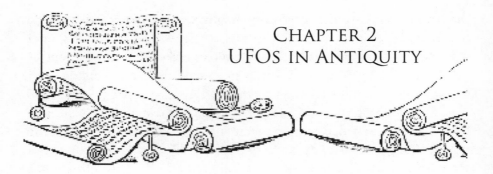

CHAPTER 2
UFOS IN ANTIQUITY

Around 400 BCE, in his book *On Nature,* the Greek philosopher Metrodorus of Chios wrote: "it seems unnatural in a whole large field to have only one shaft of wheat, and in the infinite Universe to have only one living world."[23] The Roman historian Pliny in 66 BCE wrote that a spark fell from a star and landed on the Earth until it was the size of the Moon. At that point, it hovered in the sky for a while.[24] The Roman historian Livy spoke of "phantom ships that gleamed in the sky. . ." Livy also spoke of an "Altar" which was encircled by beings in white clothing.[25]

During the siege of the city of Tyre in 322 BCE, Alexander the Great sighted the formation of "round silver shields" circling the city, enabling him to take the city by destroying the city walls with beams of light! (This story is very similar to the Old Testament story involving the City of Jericho.) It is also alleged that Alexander also witnessed "silver shields" in 322 BCE while his army was attempting to cross the Jaxartes river in India. The Italian monk Giordano Bruno wrote in his book *Del'Infinito Universo e Mondi* that in the Cosmos there must be "an infinite number of suns with planets around them."[26] Unfortunately, on February 17, 1600, during the Inquisition, he was burned on the stake for his beliefs.

In 1690, the famous Dutch physicist Christian Huygens wrote the book *Cosmotheoros.* In this book, he attempted to bridge the beliefs of the Church with the possibility of life on other worlds by writing: "Barren planets deprived of living creatures that speak most eloquently of their Divine Architect, are unreasonable, wasteful and uncharacteristic of God, who has a purpose for everything."[27] From the time of Aristotle in the 4th Century BCE until the theories of Copernicus in the 16th Century CE, the cosmos was considered by Church and State to be centered around the earth. A lone voice "crying in the wilderness" was an astronomer named Aristarchus of Samos. Aristarchus was from Alexandria, and he lived during the 3rd century.[28] It was not until another 1800 years later that Copernicus and Galileo said "amen" to Aristarchus' claim.

Even in the 16th Century, when Galileo supported the theories of Copernicus that the earth was not the center of the universe, society could not handle these findings. Galileo was treated deplorably at the hands of the gate-keepers of the status quo—the Church, more specifically, the Catholic Church. In 1633, the Church was not the least bit intrigued by Galileo's suggestion that the Bible was wrong in believing that the sun was placed in the heavens to serve the earth. Rather than listen to Galileo's message, they decided to punish him.

The old adage is true that yesterday's heresies are tomorrow's dogmas. When we challenge the ruling paradigm as Galileo did, we may go head to head with many who have vested interest in maintaining the status quo because of their positions in the existing hegemonic hierarchy. These interested parties will seek to cover up the emerging truth. These are the times when we need to remember Galileo. Yes, he was sentenced to three years imprisonment. But today we know he was correct. Acknowledging that UFO's and their occupants exist, and that they have existed since the beginning of recorded history, is the stuff of Copernicus and Galileo. According to the Roman poet Catullus, who lived from approximately 87 to 54 BCE, the writings of Homer refer to a time when the Gods from space dwelt among the heroes of old. Catullus writes, "For then, before religion was despised, the sky-dwellers in person used to visit the stainless homes of heroes and be seen at mortal gatherings."[29]

One of the earliest written records of a UFO sighting dates back to 1450 BCE. The sighting was witnessed by none other than Egyptian Pharoah Thutmose III. In the 22nd year of his reign, in the third month of winter, and the sixth hour of the day, this object was seen. According to an article by Marcus Walker in the British publication *Alien Encounters,* the story is as follows:

> . . . the scribes of the House of Life found that there was a circle
> of fire coming from the sky. It had no head. From its mouth

came a breath that stank. One rod long was its body and a rod wide, and it was noiseless. And the hearts of the scribes became terrified and confused, and they laid themselves flat on their bellies. They reported to Pharaoh...

Walker later goes on to describe the measurements of the craft. According to Walker, a rod is the equivalent of five and a half yards. This makes the body sixteen and a half feet long and the same wide. It is likely that the fuel emitted from the craft caused a vapor trail that caused the scribe of the time to note, "...from its mouth came a breath that stank."

Even the writings of Plato and Aristotle mention UFOs. Plato wrote on a myriad of subjects, including the lost continent of Atlantis. Yet Plato is rumored to have believed in his early years that the "gods" drove shining chariots across the sky.[30] Why is it that we take Plato's word regarding so many other subjects but when it comes to Atlantis and UFOs, we ignore him? The 4th Century BCE Greek philosopher Aristotle wrote of "Heavenly Discs." He mentioned a meteor that fell out of the sky at a place called Aegospotami and went on to claim that the object rose up in the wind and descended elsewhere.[31]

The books that comprise what we today refer to as the Bible are not the only sacred scriptures that speak of flying machines and their occupants. The Mayan civilization flourished in what we now call Central American and southern Mexico from roughly 300 BCE to 950 CE and mysteriously vanished without a trace. Some scholars speculate that the Mayan civilization may have existed for thousands of years prior to 300 BCE. The ancient Maya scriptures called the *Popol Vuh* (Council Book) are believed to be a collection of Mayan beliefs and legends passed down orally for centuries. The *Popol Vu*h describes the earth as round and uses a 365-day calendar, in itself an astounding mathematical achievement that bespeaks an incredible knowledge of the cosmos. The original writer of the *Popol Vuh* is unknown. Father Ximenez, a Spanish priest, translated the *Popol Vuh* from Mayan into Spanish, and the translation was published in Vienna in 1857.[32] The translation by a Spanish priest may account for presence of some Christian ideas found in the *Popol Vuh*; yet, despite the Christian influences, there is evidence that the Mayans believed in "gods from another world."

For instance, The *Popol Vuh* states that mankind has been created to be the servants of the gods. This idea is very consistent with the writings of Zecharia Sitchin. Sitchin is an ancient Near East language scholar who has studied ancient texts in their original languages. His hypothesis is that ancient astronauts created human beings to be their slaves in order to mine gold found in parts of Africa and other mineral-rich areas of planet Earth. In the *Popol Vuh*, the gods were quoted as saying: "Let us make him who shall nourish and sustain us! What shall we do to be invoked, in order to be remembered on earth? We have already tried with our first creations, our first creatures. . . so let us make them praise us. . . Let us try to make obedient, respectful beings who will nourish and sustain us."[33]

The *Popol Vuh* also states that the first human beings created were too intelligent and had too many abilities, so the gods made later humans less godlike so they would not to become a threat. In the Judeo-Christian tradition, Adam and Eve were also perceived as a threat because they had access to the tree of knowledge in the Garden of Eden. In addition, the Mayan scriptures relate the story that each god spoke a different language and that each Mayan tribe had to learn the new language when they were under the rule of a new god. The story can be juxtaposed to the biblical story about the confusion of languages and the Tower of Babel.

Scholars have often found themselves puzzled as to the source of the Mayans' precise mathematical accuracy regarding the planets and their calendar, especially without the benefit of telescopes. By acknowledging the ancient astronauts described in the *Popol Vuh*, we have an answer to those questions.

Another scriptural source for UFO activity are the Hindu Vedas. Just as the Bible does not give a one hundred percent guarantee of complete accuracy of the text, neither do the Vedas. These stories were passed down from generation to generation orally before being written down. In fact, scholars do not know exactly how old the Vedic Scriptures are. However, that need not deter one from reading and discerning these sacred texts. George King and Richard Lawrence write about the Vedic Scriptures in their book, *Contact With The Gods From Space*. King and Lawrence are both religious scholars, with advanced degrees in Divinity and Theological Studies. The authors write about a text called the Ramayana, which uses the Sanskrit word *Vimana*, defined as "flying celestial vehicle." Excerpts from their book regarding the Ramayana read:

> When morning dawned, Rama, taking the vimana Puspaka had sent him by Vivpishans, stood ready to depart. Self-propelled was that car. It was large and finely painted... That vimana, resembling a bright cloud in the sky, is in the city of Lanka.[34]

> ...He saw a very beautiful vimana coming down from the sky as if the brilliant full moon were coming down, illuminating in all directions.... While travelling through space he saw all of the planets in the solar system, and on the path he saw all the demi-gods on their vimanas showering flowers upon him like rain.[35]

The Hindu text called the Mahabharata also speaks about aerial vehicles called *Vimanas*. The Mahabharata is a text believed to have been written around 3000 BCE.[36] In Vedic scriptures, there are two kinds of vimanas, or flying machines, mentioned. The first type of craft mentioned is man-made and flies with birdlike wings. The second type of craft mentioned flies in a very mysterious manner and is not made by human beings. The beings associated with these flying vehicles in the Vedic scriptures possessed powers similar to those presently ascribed to modern day UFO visitors. In fact, the Roman writer, Flavius Philostratus describes Indian sages in his writings who, "do not fight an invader, but repel him with celestial artillery of thunder and lighting, for they are holy and saintly men."[37] The Vedas and also the Buddhist scriptures are open to life from other planets and other planetary intelligences. For instance, the Mahayana Buddhist sect is known for placing great emphasis on showing compassion to all living things. However, they also adhere to the concept that gods come down to earth from time to time throughout human history in human form! These beings are known as avatars. In a different part of the world, we find similar traditions; many Native American tribes speak of "Star People" or "Star Nations" who have traveled to this earth on flying "seed pods," introducing the tribes to fire.[38]

Considering this evidence, it is ironic that there are still many people today who refuse to believe that we may not be the only life forms in the entire universe. Unfortunately, many of these people are part of our religious, governmental, scientific, and military institutions. In a left-brained technocratic, materialistic, and science-worshipping culture such as ours, it is still inconceivable to some that there may be other civilizations in the cosmos whose technological and/or spiritual capabilities exceed ours. Is this arrogance, naiveté, stupidity, or fear? Is it all of the above? There are UFO encounters being reported today by hundreds, if not thousands, of credible people. Yet, there is another question that looms even larger for our purposes: given that the evidence suggests that these visitors have been coming to planet earth for thousands of years, what do they have to do with our present-day religions?

There has been much good that has come out of Christianity, as with all the world's religions. It must also be stated that the history of Christianity, as well as many world religions, has also been tainted by false teachings and the abuse of power. Teachings that were not consistent with the dominant hegemony were rooted out, sometimes ruthlessly so. It is also true that thousands upon thousands of years ago, humankind was not as technologically developed as we are now. There are those who would argue this point, citing the stories of Atlantis, Lemuria, and other civilizations now relegated to the margins and labeled as the mythology of primitive peoples. But even if those civilizations did exist, our biblical ancestors were certainly not privy to the wonders of the technological age. Our biblical ancestors could not imagine, much less understand, space travel or genetic engineering. When they then encountered UFOs or ETs, how might they have interpreted their experiences?

UFOs and the Old Testament
How did the prophet Isaiah know that the planet earth was indeed a sphere? Isaiah chapter 40, verse 22 states, "it is he who sits above the circle of the earth and its inhabitants are like grasshoppers." Where does the prophet get this information if allegedly the earth was thought of as flat—though the Mayans knew better—until the time of Columbus? In the book of Amos chapter five, verse 8, Amos says that "the Lord" created the Pleiades and Orion. How was Amos made aware of the star clusters Pleiades and Orion? Where was he getting his information? Perhaps he got this information from extraterrestrial spacecraft carrying beings with extraordinary abilities. Could beings from another dimension or world

have passed this information on to Amos? Perhaps our biblical ancestors were describing the visits from "angels" or "Lords" in the only way that they knew.

On page 18 of *The New York Post*, dated August 8, 1996, there was a very interesting story. A woman by the name of Mary Thompson died at the age of 120. At least this is the age her physician, Louis Murray, believed her to be. Mary Thompson was the daughter of slaves. Because she was the daughter of slaves, she had no official birth certificate. In her lifetime, Thompson saw the invention of the telephone, the first flight of the Wright brothers, as well as both world wars and the birth of jazz. Less then 24 hours before her death, Thompson gave an interview to a nurse by the name of Mary Lee Jackson at the Orlando Regional Medical Center, in Florida. Ms. Jackson quotes Thompson as having said, "She was telling me about the first time she ever saw an airplane. She said she was very frightened... *She thought it was a giant bird and she didn't realize it had a motor!*" (emphasis mine)

To the mind of those people living in biblical times who or what else could these beings be but "gods" descending from heaven to visit the earth. Famed author Erich Von Daniken in his book *Chariots Of The Gods* uses the experience of his trip to Israel on *El Al* airlines to illustrate this point.

Everyone awaited the god, whom was called "El Al," who, from the looks of it, was a mighty god indeed. I heard more voices of angels as another cherub (a very beautiful cherub) strapped me into my seat by using a broad strap around my waist. Suddenly a terrible noise, like the roaring of a violent storm occurred. The bird shook and started to move, and it roared away and left the earth faster than a gazelle. From out of the glass (or eye) of the bird I saw the grass and water below.[39]

Truly the gods of "EL AL" are mighty indeed. I think you get the point that I am attempting to make. In many instances the craft itself, as well as the occupants, were hailed and worshipped as gods. These "gods" are written and talked about by our ancestors; yet, our modern day historians, scientists, and scholars write these stories off as mythology. But have we made the mistake of misunderstanding what our ancestors were trying to tell us? They did not possess the vocabulary to express what must have been the most exhilarating, and perhaps the most bizarre event, of their primitive lifetimes.

Another example is the following scenario: That which we might recognize as a helicopter landing on a battlefield would likely have been considered a religious experience to someone 5,000 years ago, during our biblical ancestors' time.

> ... and, lo, out of the clouds came a great tribulation with a voice like the sound of rushing waters. And round about over the body was a dark cloud like a circle, which seemed to turn as it approached. When it came close upon the ground a great whirlwind went forth causing the earth and all thereabout to tremble and scatter. And when it settled upon the earth, from the bowels of tribulation, the Lord sent forth two angels. When they approached the wounded warrior who wretched in pain on the ground, he was comforted for they pierced his veins with a needle and withdrew the pain. Then, into his body they poured forth blood from heaven which was not red as blood of the flesh but was crystal clear like the blood of an angel; and therefore his life was saved.[40]

From the point of view of a man or woman in biblical times, anything that came down from the sky would be considered a god, or at least sent by the gods. Now consider what the site of modern technology, such as a helicopter or rocket ship, would do to the mind of a 1st Century man or woman. The explanation of this type of phenomenon would probably sound an awful lot like what we find in Western civilization's most sacred book—*The Bible*!

Carlo Crivelli painted the *Annunciation with Saint Emidius* in 1486. Note the disc shaped object in the sky in the space between the buildings.

The Madonna with Saint Giovannino was painted by Domenico Ghirlandaio between 1449 – 1494. To the right on the Virgin's head you will note an oblong object in the sky, and below is a man look up at the object.

GENESIS

The book of Genesis is a good place to start. Let me first begin with a definition of the word *orthodoxy*. This is important because orthodoxy is at the core of everything we are taught about science and religion. The Greek word *ortho* means straight, and the word *doxy* means teaching. The so-called "straight teaching" that we have received in our culture has deeply affected our sense of values, our sense of meaning, and our sense of selves and the world around us. We are the children of the great divorce between science and religion. Perhaps reconciliation is in order between our two "parents" if we are to begin to bear witness to the mystery of UFOs and the Bible.

The first example to start with is the *Nephilim*. Author and scholar Zecharia Sitchin is one of an extremely small group of orientalists who can read the Sumerian clay tablets that trace the events of humans on Earth from the earliest times. He was born in Russia and raised in Palestine, where he acquired a profound knowledge of modern and ancient Hebrew, other Semitic and European languages, the Old Testament, and the history of archaeology of the Near East. He describes himself as a "believing Jew." Sitchin's story starts when he was nine years old in Hebrew class in Palestine. He and his classmates were studying Noah, who he was and how he was told to build the ark. Sitchin relates the following about his experience in that class:

> My own interest in the subject goes back to my school days when studying the Bible in its original Hebrew language. The talk of the Deluge, the "Great Flood" in chapter 6 of Genesis begins by stating that "those were the days when the sons of the Elohim took the daughters of men as wives, and had children by them." The Bible calls those divine beings Nephilim [the children of the Elohim and daughters of men] and my teacher explained that the term means giants... I asked my instructor why he said the word Nephilim means "giants" when it actually means "those who have come down from heaven to earth."[41]

Sitchin was told by his instructor that you do not question the Bible. Sitchin replied that the biblical word *Nephilim*, which comes from the root *Naphal*[42] and means "to come down," actually meant those who come down from heaven to earth, not that giants were upon the earth. Sitchin was upholding the accuracy of the terminology! He was reprimanded by his instructor, and this reprimanding sent him on a life-long quest to discover the just who the *Nephilim* were, to whom was the Bible referring? Sitchin's life work concludes that the *Nephilim* are the sons of ancient astronauts and human women.

We can also ask the question, why does Genesis refer to the *Nephilim* as sons of the gods (plural) or *Elohim* (plural). The plurality of the words is certainly an aberration in a Bible devoted to monotheism. In Genesis 1:26, God says let *us* make man in *our* image! And in Genesis 11:7, the Lord again refers to itself in the plural: "Let *us* confuse their tongues." Of course, the name of the creator God in the first line of Genesis is not "Yahweh" (YHVH) but *Elohim*, a curious word. Its singular is Eloah, meaning goddess or oak tree, but in Genesis, it is given in the plural, and not only the plural but the masculine plural. A feminine word with a masculine plural usage? Why? And to whom does the word refer? Sitchin also points out another long-standing problem with the first line of Genesis. It begins with the letter Beth which is the second letter of the Hebrew alphabet, a letter that means house. According to Sitchin, something is amiss:

> A Hebrew text about creation should begin with Aleph, the first letter of the Hebrew alphabet, for three reasons. One, it is about God. Two, it is about beginnings. Three, it is customary in Hebrew writing to align not only the words with their meaning but also the letters. The first letter should be Aleph. Where did it go? Present text: "Be reshit Elohim et ha shamayim w et ha eretz." Meaning in English: "In the beginning God created the heavens and the earth." Probably original text: "Ab rashit bara Elohim, et ha shamayim w et ha eretz." Meaning in English: "The Father of beginnings created the gods, the heavens and the earth."[43]

A Major Amendment to be Sure

Another example of a problematic biblical text with regard to our exploration of UFOs and the Bible involves the story of the Tower of Babel in the book of Genesis (Genesis 11:4-5). In the texts concerning the Tower of Shinaar—the modern Iraq[44]—humans are said to have started building a "shem." The word "shem" is translated by orthodox scholars as "name" and thus gives the text this rendering: "they made a name for themselves." (Genesis 11:4) But Sitchin points out that the word "shem" can also mean a rocket of some sort. It would seem that a missile is a far more relevant device than a name if one wishes to storm the heavens.

Exodus

The beginning of the Old Testament religion is the Exodus, which introduces something resembling a space vehicle, "a pillar of cloud by day and a pillar of fire by night," that led the Hebrews out of Egypt to the Red Sea. This object hovered over the Red Sea as it parted. Afterwards, an "angel" gives the Hebrew people religious instructions. The Old Testament contains sufficient evidence that the Hebrew people were in contact with one or more extraterrestrial intelligence(s). In the book of Exodus 10:16-21, Moses watches what appears to be a craft descending on Mount Sinai:

> On the morning of the third day there were thunders and lightnings and a thick cloud upon the mountain and a very loud trumpet blast, so that all the people who were in the camp trembled... and Mount Sinai was wrapped in smoke, because the "lord" descended upon it in fire; and the smoke of a kiln, and the whole mountain quaked greatly, as the sound of the trumpet grew louder and louder... and the "lord" said to Moses, "go down and warn the people, lest they break through to the 'lord' to gaze and many of them perish.

In Exodus, "God" says to Israelites, "You have seen how I have brought you on eagle's wings and brought you to meet myself." (Exodus 19:4) In Exodus 19:9, the "Lord" said to Moses, "Lo I am coming to you in a thick cloud, that the people may hear when I speak with you, and may believe you forever." Is the book of Exodus is describing a spaceship landing in the Old Testament? Biblical scholar G. Cope Schelhorn analyzed that scene with Moses on Mount Sinai in his book *Extraterrestrials in Biblical Prophesy* as follows:

> The main rockets make tremendous noise in their descent. The people looking upward see exhaust, fire and smoke, "thunders and lightnings." A cloud of particles and smoke reaches skyward. Noise resembling a trumpet blast is heard, either caused by retrorockets or the communication loudspeaker we later find mentioned in Ezekiel (Ezekiel 1:25, 9:1) and John (Revelations 1:10). "The Lord descended upon it (Mt. Sinai or Mt. Horeb) in fire; and the smoke went up like smoke of a kiln…" For a moment, Mt. Sinai looks from a great distance like an erupting volcano. The mountain quaked greatly.[45]

There is no reason to expect that the people who lived in biblical times called a flying saucer a "flying saucer." It is oftentimes referred to as a "cloud," but that is not to imply that biblical people actually believed that clouds carried people into space. However, it does suggest that they could only describe what they saw in the vernacular or vocabulary of the times of which they lived. I am speaking about people who lived before Copernicus. I am speaking about people who did not know that the earth was round. I am speaking about a very primitive and superstitious society, a society in which those people unfortunate enough to have epilepsy were believed to have been possessed by "demons." In this society, anything which came down from the sky—a meteor, a falling star, etc.—was considered either a sign from the "gods" or maybe even the god or gods in person.

The point should also be stressed that just as we in our present culture have shortened the phrase "unidentified flying object" to "UFO", the word "cloud" is much easier to use than "Pillar of cloud by day, and the pillar of fire by night" (Exodus13:21, 22). But what exactly did this rag-tag group of ex-slaves actually see? How does a biblical UFO encounter compare with modern sightings of UFO?

It has often been reported that in modern day sightings, UFOs exhibit a corona effect, which results in a white cloudlike halo appearance.

These craft are also reported to glow in the dark, as a "pillar of fire by night" appears to do. Yet, there is another intriguing possibility in the translation of the Hebrew term for "pillar." According to the Rev. Dr. Barry Downing, retired pastor of the Northminster Presbyterian Church in Endwell, New York and author of several books on the subject of UFOs and the Bible, the New Revised Standard Version of Bible translates two different Hebrew words as "pillar." These Hebrew words are *ammud* and *mazzebah*. Downing writes:

> In this passage, the word *ammud* is used, which may mean a cylindrical column; thus the implication would seem to be that this UFO looked like a cylindrical column (height and weight not specified), cloudlike during the day, but glowing in the dark. It is not clear whether the "pillar of cloud" stood vertical before the people or traveled horizontally to the ground.[46]

The passage again. . . the people looking upward see exhaust fire and smoke thunders and lightnings. A cloud of particles and smoke reaches skyward. Noise resembling a trumpet blast is heard, either caused by retrorockets or loudspeaker. For a moment, Mount Sinai looks from a great distance like an erupting volcano. The mountain quaked greatly. Moses speaks and God answered him in thunder. . . Here truly is a picture of a sky god descending.

Later in the book of Exodus (34:5), Moses meets the "Lord" on Mount Sinai: "And the Lord descended in the cloud, and stood with him there, and proclaimed the name of the Lord." Yet, something else very significant also happens to Moses. After being face to face with "God," Exodus verses 29-30 describes something very interesting:

> And it came to pass, when Moses came down from Mount Sinai, with the two tablets of testimony in Moses' hand, that Moses did not know that the skin of his face shone while he talked with him. And when Aaron and all the children of Israel saw Moses, behold the skin of his face shone, and they were afraid to come nigh him.

If Moses' face had shone from joy after being in the presence of the Most High, why were people afraid of him? It appears that he may also have been exposed to extremely high levels of radiation. Perhaps, he was actually taken aboard the vessel. In any case, thereafter Moses had to wear a veil around in his face in the presence of his people. The only time he removed the veil was when he was speaking to the Lord. (See Exodus 34:31-35).

The story is all the more fascinating when one considers that the Israelites did not really have a "Hebrew" religion until after their exodus from Egypt. According to the story, after the Pharaoh frees the Hebrew slaves in Egypt, he has a change of heart. Pharaoh decides to retrieve his slaves, only to find out that they are being led in the wilderness by "the Lord" (Exodus 13:17-18), a "Lord" who is leading them by day in a "pillar of cloud" and by night by a "pillar of fire." The book of Exodus tells us that that Moses was a man with great respect in the eyes of the Egyptians (Exodus 11:3). However, there is an interesting plot twist to this story of the Hebrew Exodus. On numerous occasions the "Lord"—Jehovah or Yahweh—sent Moses to tell Pharaoh to, "Let my people go." Not only does Jehovah promise to liberate the Hebrews from the tyrannical rule of the Pharaoh, Jehovah says that he will harden Pharaoh's heart in order to prove a point. The Egyptian King refuses time and time again to heed the warning of Moses and Jehovah, thus providing Jehovah the opportunity to show his power. This self-proclaimed jealous "god" uses his power to cause the Nile River to turn to blood, depriving men, women, and children drinking water and fish for food. A plague of insects (locusts and flies) covers the land of Egypt, not to mention severe hailstorms and frogs also covering the land.

There was also a terrible pestilence that killed domestic animals, the killing of the first-born child of the Egyptians, as well as an illness that consisted of festering boils on the bodies of the Egyptians. As if that were not enough, after Pharaoh cries "uncle" and decides to release the Hebrew slaves, Jehovah has decided once again to display his egotistical powers of persuasion. We read in Exodus 14:4 that Jehovah says, "...I will make Pharaoh obstinate, and he will pursue them (the Hebrews), so that I may win glory for myself at the expense of Pharaoh and his army..." During this time, Jehovah is guiding the Hebrew people in "the pillar of cloud by day and the pillar of fire by night." (At this rate, one may begin to ask if Jesus came to save us from ourselves or from "gods" like Jehovah.) The question then becomes, just who or what is "Yahweh," the Hebrew "Lord?"

YAHWEH

Yahweh's moods seem all too human to be viewed as an omnipotent deity. He is often jealous, angry, or surly. At times, his behavior is just plain outrageous. One example is Leviticus 27:3-8. Here we have the "Lord" advising Moses on how much to charge for male slaves, and some of these people are mere children!

Yahweh is the form of the name of God used in the Old Testament of the Bible. God revealed this personal name to Moses in an earlier form as YHWH. Jewish scholars called *Masoretes*, who worked for over four hundred years on the reproduction of the original Hebrew Old Testament, introduced the name Yahweh by adding vowels.[47] The familiar name Jehovah is an English translation of Yahweh.

Scripture is replete with verses in which human emotions are attributed to Yahweh. Grief and sorrow are among these, for example, Genesis 6:5-6 reads, "the Lord saw that the wickedness of humankind was great in the earth, and that every inclination of the thoughts of their hearts was only evil continually. And the Lord was sorry that he had made humankind on the earth, and it grieved him to his heart." There was certainly no lack of things that Yahweh hated. For instance, in Zechariah 8:17, we read, "Do not devise evil in your hearts against one another, and love no false oath, for all these are things that I hate, says the Lord." The prophet Amos records the words of Yahweh to the people of Israel: "I hate, I despise your feast days" (Amos 5:21). And in Isaiah 1:14, "your new moons and appointed feast days my soul hates." In Deuteronomy 4:23, "Nor shall you set up a stone pillar (craven image)—things that the Lord your God hates." Psalm 5:5-6 speaks of Yahweh's hatred of evil people for the psalmist wrote, "The boastful will not stand before your eyes, your hate and wrath."

Yahweh unleashes his wrath in order to correct, guide, and teach the people of Israel. Aside from the antics described earlier such killing the first-born children of Egypt and hardening the Pharaoh's heart to prove a point, here are a few more examples. Exodus 33:5: "For the Lord said to

Moses, say to the Israelites, You are a stiff-necked people; If for a single moment I should go among you, I would consume you." Exodus 22:2: "If you do abuse them, when they cry out to me, I will surely heed their cry; my wrath will burn, and I will kill you with the sword, and your wives shall become widows and your children orphans."

Yet there were times in the Exodus story when Yahweh exhibited restraint and even love. For instance, this passage from the books of Jeremiah and Hosea: "I have loved you [Israel] with an everlasting love, therefore I have continued my faithfulness to you" (Jeremiah 33:3). "How can I hand you over O Israel? How can I treat you like Zeboim? My heart recoils within me; my compassion grows warm and tender. I will not execute my fierce anger" (Hosea 11:8-9).

It is quite evident that Yahweh grieved, repented, loved, hated, and was merciful. He was a jealous "God" who kept his promises; he was a consuming fire of wrath and a practicer of swift and lethal revenge. The ancient writers recorded the entire gauntlet of human emotions attributed to Yahweh. However, Yahweh himself set the record straight on his overall similarity to human beings when he said, "for my thoughts are not your thoughts, nor are your ways my ways… For as the heavens are higher than the earth, so are my ways higher than your ways and my thoughts than your thoughts" (Isaiah 55:8-9).

What are we to make of this god called Yahweh? His emotions are all too human to be considered an omnipotent deity. He is a process theologian's dream. Yahweh does seem to mellow as the story of his relationship with the people of Israel progresses. It is my contention that this Yahweh is an astronaut from space whom the people of Israel worshipped as a deity. The commandment to not have any other god before Yahweh, to my mind, speaks quite clearly to the fact that there was indeed competition from *other gods or astronauts being worshipped by other tribes at that time!* It is rather common knowledge that the Israelites were not always a monotheistic people, even after their exodus from Egypt. Perhaps it would be interesting to entertain the idea that, much like the man we call Jesus today, Yahweh could also make the claim: "I am not of this world" (John 8:23).

OLD TESTAMENT PROPHETS, UFOS, AND ALIENS

There is evidence of UFO activity surrounding the life of Elijah, the prophet. When Elijah's earthly mission is complete, we read that, "The Lord was about to take Elijah up to heaven in a whirlwind" (2 Kings 2:1). The Bible tells us that Elijah and his companion Elisha were walking together, "and as they still went on and talked, behold a chariot of fire and horses of fire separated the two of them (a fiery chariot can be interpreted as a UFO as well) and Elijah went up by a whirlwind into heaven" (2 Kings 2:11). The text also makes clear that there were fifty witnesses to Elijah's flight heavenward.

The book of the prophet Ezekiel also contains UFO sightings and contact with ET intelligences. Ezekiel was a rabbi and a prisoner of King Nebuchadnezzar during the Babylonian Exile in 586 BCE. Ezekiel tells what he witnessed in chapter 1, verses 4-28. His technical vocabulary was insufficient, and he had to be creative if he was to communicate exactly what it was that he saw. Ezekiel saw the commander of a ship and was convinced that the being or angel is "the Lord" (Ezekiel 9:4). In chapter 3:22-24, we read that, "The hand of the Lord was there upon me; and he said to me, arise, go forth into the plain and there I will speak with you." It seems from the text that Ezekiel was transported somewhere by some object in the sky. We read in chapter 3:12-15:

> Then the spirit lifted me up, and as the glory of the Lord rose from its place, there I heard behind me the sound of loud rumbling. It was the sound of the wings of the living creatures brushing up against one another, and the sound of the wheels beside them, that sounded like loud rumbling. The spirit lifted me up and bore me away; I went in bitterness in the heat of my spirit, the hand of the Lord being strong upon me. I came to the exiles at Tel-Abib, who lived by the river Chebar. And I sat there among them stunned for seven days.

It Would Appear that Ezekiel was given a Brief Introductory Flight and then Returned Home.

Josef Blumrich was formerly employed as a NASA engineer. His official title was Chief of the Systems Layout Branch for NASA. In 1974, Mr. Blumrich authored a book entitled *The Spaceships of Ezekiel*. In this book, Mr. Blumrich actually includes a rendering of a spaceship from the information provided by the prophet Ezekiel from the Bible. Mr. Blumrich stated, "at all times, we must remember that Ezekiel does not interpret what he sees because he cannot interpret it."[48] It would be as if a Neanderthal man or woman were to attempt to describe a helicopter sighting. Yet Blumrich used the first chapter of Ezekiel, verses 1-28, and designed the spacecraft that the prophet saw.

The prophet Enoch also describes a scenario in which he saw a being and assumed that the being was either an angel or the "Lord." The Book of Enoch was discovered in Egypt in 1773. Because of its content, the early Church Bishops excluded the Book of Enoch from the original canon. The questionable content describes the ascent of Enoch through the heavens on what appears to have been a spaceship! No doubt verses such as this one were too controversial for the Church Fathers; Enoch describes his vision thus: "And the vision was shown to me, behold, in the vision clouds invited me and a mist summoned me, and the course of the stars and the lightnings sped me, and the winds in the vision caused me to fly and lifted me upward and bore me into heaven" (Enoch 14:8-25).

What happened here? The phrases "clouds invited me" and "a mist summoned me" suggest not only smoke caused by the engine, but are also reminiscent of present-day eyewitness accounts of UFO sightings. Some present-day sightings suggest that UFOs often use clouds cover, either appearing out of them or somehow creating a cloud cover for themselves. One thing is certain; Enoch was flying. He was moving very fast; for he wrote, "the course of the stars and lighting sped and hastened me, something has lifted me upward". Enoch was taken up into space.

The prophet Zechariah described his experiences in the book by the same name, chapter 5: 1-2: "Then I turned and lifted up my eyes and looked, and behold a flying scroll. And he said unto me, What do you see? I answered, I see a flying scroll the length thereof is 20 cubits, its width 10 cubits. . ." A scroll may just happen to be a cigar-shaped spacecraft. The first few verses in chapter 6 of Zechariah give evidence of UFO activity as well. In the first verse, the writer spoke of seeing four chariots coming out of two mountains (motherships?) made of bronze. In verse seven, the commander of the ship, also referred to as "the Lord," tells the chariots to "go and patrol the earth." It is curious that "the Lord" needed to send out patrols to watch over the planet.

Angels or Aliens?

Do not neglect to show hospitality to strangers, for by doing so some have entertained angels unawares.
Hebrews 13:2

The Bible speaks of a divine world that includes angels up in the sky above the earth. Sometimes the angels appear as messengers who come from above; yet, no mention is ever made of them having wings. What do they look like? According to the scriptures, some of these beings appear to look very similar to human beings. In Genesis 18:1-5, Abraham entertains three *men*. When he first encounters them, Abraham runs toward the three men and bows down as if he recognizes them and gives them reverence. He treats them with hospitality, which was the custom of the day. They have their feet washed by Abraham and their bellies filled. He also recognized them as being messengers of God. These "men" proceed to tell his wife Sarah that although she has gone through what we today call menopause, she will become pregnant. They possess the gift of telepathy and read Sarah's thoughts, before going on their way. Later, just as they predicted, Sarah does conceive a son whose name is Isaac. In Genesis 18:13, one of the "men" is referred to as "the Lord." No mention is made of these "men" having wings; instead they appear quite human.

From the book of Genesis basically through the book of Revelations, God is usually an invisible deity who uses messengers called "angels" to carry out his orders. Christian artists usually depicted angels as beings with wings; yet, the above Bible passage clearly demonstrates that Abraham believed these "angels" to be human beings. My point is that the Bible does not indicate that angels are easily recognized, since they do not have wings. The most obvious question then is how do they get here? It would seem that they have some sort of transportation system that is referred to either as a cloud, a chariot of fire, or a vehicle that can fly, looking like a cloud during the day and glowing like fire in the dark.

One must be careful lest we generalize that all extraterrestrial beings look alike. There are modern day reports of ETs with a myriad of descriptions. Some are described as "grays" with large heads and slanted eyes, some are reptilian-looking beings, some beings resemble the "praying mantis" insect, and some are blue-haired blue-eyed beings that look like the Eurocentric images of Jesus.[49] Many of these beings appear more humanoid than human from modern day witnesses.

Scientific Christians may or may not believe in angels, but do not be deceived. There are many sincere and educated Christians who believe in the literal existence of angels. The Rev. Dr. Billy Graham, in an interview with David Frost, conceded as much on national television when he publicly discussed the *possibility* of extraterrestrial life.[50] Dr. Graham stated publicly that there was absolutely no doubt in his mind that angels actually existed. Dr. Graham wrote in his book *Angels:*

> Some Christian writers have speculated that UFOs could well be part of God's host who preside over the physical affairs of universal creation. While we cannot assert such a view with certainty, many people are now seeking some type of supernatural explanation for these with greater frequency around the entire world and in unexpected places... Sincere Christians, whose views are anchored in a strong commitment to Scriptures contend that UFOs are angels. But are they? These people point to certain passages. . . Any attempt to connect such passages with the visits of angels may, at best, be speculation. What is interesting, however, is that such theories are now being given serious attention by people who make no claim to believe in the God of the Bible.[51]

The point is that there may be several different types of extraterrestrials who have visited our planet since historic—and even prehistoric—times.

None of these beings were reported to have wings of any kind. Some Christians will admit that the Bible believes in some kind of "heavenly beings," but they may not take this belief literally. They may concede that the biblical writers themselves may have believed in these beings, but surely not educated Christians. Yet for some strange reason, conservative Christians want their angels to be every bit as real as the Bible makes them out to be, to sit down and have a meal with Abraham, but those same Christians often do not want them flying around in UFOs, being chased by United States Air Force jets.

To reiterate, angels (or aliens) in the Bible are not dressed in wings. The scripture that says, "do not neglect to show hospitality to strangers, for thereby some have entertained angels unawares" (Hebrews 13:2), is based on the assumption that angels indeed look very human. According to modern day contactees, that may not always be the case, since the humanoid-looking "grays" are the most readily depicted in our culture as representing all ET life forms.

While the modern ET visitors and the angels in the Bible may not look alike, angels in the Bible are noted for their ability to read minds (telepathy) and to bring about pregnancy (Genesis 18)[52]. Angels can be visible or invisible to humans when humans are in a trance state or dreaming (Genesis 15:12 and 28:12). Many of these same experiences have been reported by modern day contactees. Unfortunately, modern day contactees rarely get support from their religious communities. While churches can embrace the experiences described in the Bible, they often ignore, trivialize, or treat as a manifestation of the demonic similar experiences in modern times. This should come as no surprise, for as a species, we human beings are infamous for fearing and demonizing that which we do not understand.

There are not many clergy who will acknowledge the existence of UFOs or their occupants. Fear of ridicule, of course, comes into play, but it is also true that the mind does not easily fathom such topics. The majority of conservative religious writers and clergy take the literal meaning of the scriptures very seriously but do not want to even consider the UFO hypothesis. In other words, they take the stories literally but do not want anyone to even suggest just how the events described in the Bible might have taken place. For some conservatives, however, the topic of UFOs in the Bible is taken seriously. Although for these people, the ETs found in the Judeo-Christian scriptures are agents of the devil. Books such as *The Millennial Deception* by Timothy Dailey, *Alien Encounters* by Chuck Missler and Mark Eastman, and *UFOs and the Alien Agenda* by Bob Larsen are all written by conservative biblical authors.[53]

The more liberal religious writers and clergy often approach the biblical stories as mere allegory and metaphor, rather than literally. Therefore, most liberal clergy and writers do not examine the biblical text for indications of a UFO or extraterrestrial presence.

JESUS AND THE UFO CONNECTION

Let us now turn our attention to the life and ministry of the man known in our Western culture as Jesus. There can be little doubt, after examining the evidence, that UFOs and their occupants took great interest in the life of the man Jesus. His question to his disciples in the Gospel of Luke (9:18) still looms large for us in today's fast-paced technological world. Jesus' question echoes down the corridors of time, reverberating to our modern ears.

JESUS OF NAZARETH: WHO DO YOU SAY THAT I AM?

Both the first and second testaments of the Bible tell us of a world of angels and demons, flying chariots and clouds. This was the world of Jesus of Nazareth, as well, so it is only fitting that we ask ourselves, who was this Jesus? (Indeed Jesus himself was quite curious as to what the answer to this question might be for he inquired of his disciples in Luke 9:18-20, "Whom do the people say that I am?") Who was Jesus? Prophet, ethical teacher, Rabbi, savior of the world, Son of the Most High God. For some, Jesus and the God of creation are one. For many people, Jesus is all of the above and much more besides. To others, Jesus was quite simply a human being who lived an exemplary life.

Some two thousand years after his birth, we are still faced with the enigma of the true identity of Yeshua Ben Yosef (his Hebrew name, Joshua son of Joseph). Nevertheless, whoever or whatever we believe this Jesus to be, one thing is certain; this man so influenced human history on this planet that many of us now divide that history into BC (before the birth of "Christ") and AD (after his death and resurrection). Biblical scholars continue their search for the so-called historical Jesus, in an attempt to separate the Jesus of history from the Christ of faith. No one in the history of the world has drawn so much attention. Jesus is an icon for the ages.

I will attempt in this section to show the relation of the UFO phenomenon and other cosmic anomalies to the life of Jesus. These events may possibly give us a clue as to who this man actually was. I will refrain from giving a chronological sequence of the Christian faith, but instead I will examine the most obvious connections between the Gospels and UFO activity. The birth of Jesus has been connected to UFO activity in the Gospel narratives. Jesus, like Gautuma Siddhartha (five hundred years before Jesus) also known as "the Buddha," has significant astral events surrounding his birth. A bright light is said to have illuminated the world on the night of his birth to mark the holy event. It appears that in the ancient world, the birth of special persons was often seen as marked by astral events, such as a bright light or an auspicious alignment of a constellation with the planets.[54] It is also interesting to note that the birth narratives of both Jesus and Buddha have their respective mothers conceive without the benefit of normal human intercourse.[55]

THE STAR OF BETHLEHEM

The book of Matthew, chapter 2, verses 9-11, reads as follows:

> And Lo, the star which they saw in the east went before them, till it came and stood over where the young child was. When they saw the star, they rejoiced exceedingly with great joy. And when they were come into the house, they saw the young child with Mary, his mother and fell down and worshipped him.

In all likelihood, if we are to take the story literally, this "star" was in fact a UFO. Stars do not travel across the sky and hover over mangers or stables, or anything else for that matter. Nor do stars shine lights down on the surface of the earth. If a star had in fact moved through the heavens and stopped, the gravitational field of our entire solar system would have been in disarray, which would, in turn, have precipitated a horrific disaster on earth and possibly on other planets as well. Given that, the most obvious question to ask is why would an extraterrestrial intelligence be so concerned about the birth and the welfare of this child?

We find that in the story of Abraham and Sarah in Genesis, in the story of Samson in the book of Judges (13:4), as well as in the birth of John the Baptist by his mother Elizabeth, "God" appears preoccupied with women who are "barren" and their male offspring. Jesus' mother may or may not have been a virgin in the traditional sense of the word, for the Hebrew word *alma* means young maiden. "Young maiden" does not necessarily mean one who had not engaged in intercourse.

Regarding the identity of biblical angels, it has been suggested that if we were to replace the word "angel" with the word "extraterrestrial or alien" in this story, or any other biblical story, these stories take on a whole new meaning. Let us experiment by reading the story of the exchange between Samson's mother (who is nameless and only referred to as Manoah's wife) and the "angel' very carefully. "And the angel of the Lord appeared unto the woman, and said unto her, behold now thou art barren and bearest not, but thou shall conceive, and bear a son... For the child shall be a Nazarene unto God from the womb, and he shall deliver Israel out of the hands of the Philistines." (Judges 13:5) The angel (alien) impregnates Manoah's wife and creates a hybrid with super-human abilities. Whether they make love the old-fashioned way or not is not specified, though I somehow doubt it. The Old Testament story of Abraham and Sarah in the book of Genesis 18:9-10 is very similar to the story of Manoah and his wife.

There is no doubt that Jesus possessed super-human qualities on a spiritual level that Samson did not possess, but they are both "special" because of their births. This leads to more inquiries and speculation about the story of the virgin birth in the New Testament. Is this story actually a story involving artificial insemination? The mother of Jesus had an experience with an angel similar to that of Manoah's wife. Mary was not barren, but she could have maintained her "virgin status" through artificial insemination by an ET.

In his thought provoking book, *The Gods Of Eden*, author William Bramley wrote: "To someone engaging in artificial insemination, there would be a practical reason... artificial insemination helps guarantee control over the physical characteristics of a future baby, something which cannot be assured in random human mating."[56] This is certainly not to say that the mother of Jesus could not have been impregnated "the old fashioned way."[57] Yet, the fact remains that the Bible tells us that Mary was not impregnated by a human man in the case of Jesus' birth. A child with only one human parent is only half-human! In fact, an angel of the Lord appears to Joseph, Jesus' earthly father to inform him not to fear because all is in divine order, and that Mary is indeed a key component in a cosmic plan.

There is no doubt that Jesus was "special" to say the least. In the Book of Antiquities, written by the Jewish historian Josephus, we can glean another clue as to the identity and power of this Jesus. In book 18, chapter 3, verse 63, Josephus writes:

> Now there was about this time, Jesus, a wise man, *if it be lawful to call him a man, for he was a doer of many wonderful works*—a teacher of such men receive the truth with pleasure. He drew over to him both many of the Jews, and many of the Gentiles. He was [the] Christ; and when Pilate, at the suggestion of

the principal men amongst us, had condemned him to the cross, those who loved him at first did not forsake him, for he appeared to them alive again on the third day, as the divine prophets had foretold these and ten thousand other wonderful things concerning him; and the tribe of Christians, so named from him, are not extinct to this day.[58]

What is it about Jesus that gives Josephus pause to ponder whether or not it is even appropriate to call Jesus a man? Was Jesus one of the celestial sons from above? Obviously he was considered by some, then and now, to be a god or God from above in human form. Perhaps his uniqueness stems from his father being an ET/angel from the heavens. Given the evidence thus far, this many not be as far-fetched as it first appears. Jesus' powers no doubt were given to him from above, as he acknowledges before Pilate in John's Gospel. How else can a first century person make sense of the miracles and mighty works that Jesus performed?

In later life, Jesus frequently prays to his heavenly father using the Hebrew word *abba*, which means father. And why not? His father quite literally resides in the heavens above, and quite possibly on a UFO. Jesus also says that in his father's house there are many mansions. Could Jesus possibly be hinting that the universe is his father's "house" and that the "many mansions" may be other planets? When questioned by the Pharisees, Jesus tells them, "you are from below, I am from above." Even when he is on trial for his life, he informs Pilate that any authority that Pilate might seem to have over him is given him from above. He later goes on to tell Pilate that he is in fact a king, but that his kingdom is not of this world. Finally, after his resurrection, the Bible tells us that Jesus is taken away from his disciples on a "cloud" into heaven.

THE TRANSFIGURATION

One of the most extraordinary UFO incidents in the Bible is found in the book of Matthew 17:1-8. It is called the Transfiguration of Jesus. The story goes as follows: Shortly before Jesus turns his face towards Jerusalem, his trial and subsequent crucifixion, Peter, James, John, and Jesus ascended a very high mountain (many UFO episodes take place on or near mountains). Quite unexpectedly, Jesus was transformed before their very eyes. We are told that his face shone like the sun (much like the story of Moses after seeing "the Lord"). His garments became as white as pure light; Moses and Elijah appear and converse with Jesus. The disciples ask Jesus if they should pitch tents for their guest, when out of nowhere, they hear a voice from above saying, "this is my beloved son with whom I am well pleased, listen to him." The disciples fall on their faces in awe, and, I would imagine, some fear and trepidation. Afterward, Jesus tells them to rise and to have no fear, and when they look up, Jesus is standing alone.

First, the scenario is indeed mind-boggling, considering the fact that Moses had allegedly been dead for hundreds of years. Elijah was said to have never died but instead taken up into heaven in a fiery chariot (UFO) in the midst of witnesses who were all dead and gone by the time of Jesus. The Rev. Barry Downing writes in his grounding-breaking book, *The Bible and Flying Saucers*: "The fact that Moses and Elijah were supposedly present at the transfiguration obviously points to the unity between the Old and New Testaments, as does the presence of the UFO."[59] The next question that arises for us is then, what does all of this mean for Christianity (and Judaism) in our society today?

IF UFOs ARE REAL, WHAT DOES THIS MEAN FOR THE JUDEO-CHRISTIAN BIBLICAL DOCTRINE?

When we think about the above question, we have to keep in mind that the Judeo-Christian paradigm, and its first cousin Islam, dominate the West and not the East. The worldview of Hinduism and Buddhism and much of Asia and Africa are quite different. In some ways the Hindu worldview—the view that of all of creation are varied manifestations of the divine—makes the existence of UFOs less problematic because UFOs are also part of creation and, therefore, are linked to the divine.

For instance, W. Raymond Drake, in his book, *Gods and Spacemen in the Ancient East*, quotes from this Sanskrit poem from India which may date as far back as 1400 BCE:

> Bright immortals robed in sunlight sailed across the liquid sky, and their gleaming cloud borne chariots rests on the turrets high, Ida, adja, homa offerings pleased the 'Shining Ones' on

high, Brahmans pleased with costly presents with their blessings filled the sky."[60]

Given what we know about UFOs and their occupants—that their occupants are quite capable of entering our homes at night, as well as taking us with them, reading our thoughts, and at times also influencing them—we cannot rule out the possibility that UFOs were involved in the development of the Hindu religion, or in Buddha's spiritual development. I am not an Eastern religious scholar, so I will refrain from attempting to further speculate what UFOs might mean for these Eastern religious traditions.

For now, I believe that it is safe to say that UFOs appear to be more of a problem for the Judeo-Christian tradition. Most scientific and religious literature in the West does not address the issue of UFOs. On this both science and religion agree; UFOs are a drunken relative that we would do well never to speak of in public.

Traditional Christians are used to believing that God chose to have as son born in a physical body, to live in the Middle East for approximately 33 years, and to die by crucifixion. The Romans performed this shameful act, as this was all part of God's plan, and all those unfortunate souls who happened to be born before this event took place, or choose to believe otherwise, have missed out on salvation and will in all probability burn in hell. This type of mentality must change if Christianity is to remain relevant in the 21st Century and beyond. Our way of doing "God Talk" will have to change. Of course, words can only get in the way in the finite attempts to know or to articulate the infinite, but try we must.

Mystics from various traditions have attempted to teach us that there is a universal connection among all things. Science has reached the same conclusion. This connection has various names; some may label it the soul-force, cosmic intelligence, God, infinite mind, etc. Others may call it love. Science often refers to it as energy. Label it what we will, giving a name to the nameless often creates a stumbling block that trips many people up. We think that if something has a name that it has an identity. An identity implies attributes, so we believe that we know something about it. This is a mistake. For thousands of years, this mistake has been ingrained in the human psyche. The word "God" suggests an embodiment of something that can be grasped. We have given a name to the Unknown and Unknowable and then spent endless hours trying to know it. We often try precisely because we have given it a name, but we must always fail because it is intrinsically unknowable.

The UFO phenomenon must force us to rethink our concept of the sacred. To the ancients, these beings were truly gods. We have achieved so much because of technological advancements that the ancients might consider us gods today. Despite the human proclivity for insufferable hubris, we would have to admit that the ancients would be incorrect in so naming us.

The technological and spiritual accomplishments of the "gods" boggle the mind and dwarf our so-called knowledge of how the universe works. Yet, we know that ETs are not gods. Our androcentric concepts of the divine are old and tired. This is not to say that there is no such thing as a supreme or first cause of creation. However, it is fair to say that when we admit how little we actually know about this thing we call "God," we open ourselves to endless possibilities. We as human beings are not too great at living with the questions, and it is certainly not an easy thing to do. There are always more questions than answers, yet for now, the questions are much more important than the answers.

Wislawa Szymborska is not only a gifted poet, she was the 1996 Nobel Prize Winner for Literature. In her Nobel acceptance speech, Ms. Szymborska discussed those among us who find it difficult to live with the questions in life; those among us who cannot simply say, "I do not know." She stated:

> . . . knowledge that doesn't lead to new questions quickly dies out. It fails to maintain the temperature required for sustaining life. In the most extreme cases, well known from ancient and modern history, it even poses a lethal threat to society. This is why I value that little phrase, 'I don't know,' so highly. It's small, but it expands our lives to include spaces within us as well as the outer expanses in which our tiny earth hangs suspended.[61]

There is much we do not know, but there are some things that are knowable. One of those knowable things is the existence of ET life, as well as the acceptance of that existence. The near-term implications of a government disclosure of the existence of ET life would obviously affect our geopolitical and philosophical worldview. I believe that this can be done without demonizing or deifying ET civilizations. My remarks will be brief on this issue, as my main focus is on the Judeo-Christian repercussions of such a disclosure. However, on the geopolitical front, the altering of the fundamental paradigm—about how we view ourselves as human beings, the universe, and our place in it—would be remarkably profound to say the least. Such a paradigm shift may take decades or centuries before we fully realize that we are one people on spaceship earth, among many worlds inhabited by other intelligent, and perhaps, more advanced life forms. Perhaps this realization will lessen the balkanization of our current global geopolitical structures. The differences and conflict surrounding the various racial, religious, ethnic, and national identities may well be seen in a softer light. At least this is my prayer.

The belief in UFOs in the Bible is a statement of faith, and the alleged participation of ETs in biblical stories is still yet a hypothesis. It is a challenge to the way the Bible is traditionally understood, and the claim that revelations through UFOs and ETs have continued up to the present age contradicts the common Christian belief that revelation came to an end with the New Testament. This belief also requires radical rethinking of the traditional Christian doctrines of creation and redemption.

As an example, belief in the phenomenon of UFOs and ETs in the Bible necessitates a rethinking of the New Testament account of the story of the "virgin birth"—a Christian belief that is itself imbedded in the early Christian creeds. The "virgin birth" has been interpreted in various ways by Christian theologians and social scientists alike. In traditional Christian theology, it often stands as a sign of God's intervention into human history, not to mention proof of the divinity of Jesus. However, some ufologists see it as an example of technological intervention by beings from outer space; hence, the theory of the sperm of a creature (angel) from another world or planet. In this theory, Mary can still be said to be literally a virgin, though no miracle or supernatural intervention occurred.

UFO writers and scholars have different theories as to the role that ETs might have played in the creation, evolution, and development of the human species. One position is that ETs actually created human beings. *Chariots of the Gods*, by Erich Von Daniken, may be the most well-known attempt to create a worldview in which ETs play the leading role in the evolution and development of humanity. His efforts to use scientific evidence, technological inventions, and archeological findings to support his theory have fallen on deaf ears within the scientific community. R. L. Dione's books, *Does God Drive a Flying Saucer?* and *Is God Supernatural?*, provide many illustrations as to how the UFO theory can be used to reinterpret traditional religious tenets in a more scientific manner. In response to these books, author John Saliba wrote:

> God becomes an astronaut, a superior being who lives in a more advanced civilization in some other far-away galaxy. Divine revelation is nothing but teachings from space creatures and miracles are awesome interventions by intelligences who are technologically superior to the human race. The supernatural in this view is reduced to the super-technological. God is a super-humanoid creature living on another planet. He has made himself immortal through technology and has created the human race on earth for his amusement.[62]

My problem with the assessment by Mr. Salibla is threefold. First, as I have attempted to emphasize, belief in the UFO phenomenon does not negate belief in a Supreme Creator. Perhaps this Creator created other life forms as well as human beings. Belief in the UFO phenomenon in the Bible need not trivialize "God" to the role of astronaut, in my opinion. The teacher Jesus reminds us that in his Father's house, there are many mansions (John 14:2), and there are sheep of other folds (John 10:16). Second, Mr. Salibla maintains an anthropomorphic identity for this "God" and continues to refer to "God" as male. Finally, the so-called miracles of the Bible may not be the product of super-technological know-how on the part of the ETs; perhaps the ETs are spiritually advanced as well and have an awareness of cosmic laws that we humans do not. Demonstration of these cosmic laws would surely seem to be miracles to the individuals living in biblical times, and I dare say would still appear as miracles to our 21st Century minds.

In contrast to Mr. Salibla, I believe that the theories of Von Daniken and Dione are examples of both the secularization and the recreation of the myths of the Bible. These theories secularize religion because they remove the supernatural elements of the biblical narratives. The miraculous in the scriptures becomes merely the activities of super-human beings from another planet who possess superior technological and psychic powers. "God" becomes merely a technician or scientist. The theories simultaneously recreate the myths because they introduce an element of new mystery and new material—mystery and material that forms a new paradox—paradox being the heart of all religious traditions. I believe that the majority of Christians will reject these approaches. Further, some Christians who do accept the UFO phenomenon may simply incorporate it into a paradigm of good versus evil in the universe.

UFOs as Angels or Demons: What does this mean for Christianity?

The question then arises as to whether these beings are angelic or demonic in their intent and whether they can be linked with apocalyptic times. As I mentioned, it has been my personal experience that those writers or clergy who are more conservative or evangelical theologically and who do acknowledge the ET presence in the scriptures tend to label the ETs as demonic.

Dr. Donald P. Coverdell, ThD, author of *Mystery Clouds*, devotes his entire book to describing the ETs as satanic or apocalyptic. Authors such as Bob Larson (*The Alien Agenda*), Timothy Dailey (*The Millennial Deception*), and Chuck Missler and Mark Eastman (*Alien Encounters*) follow the same line of reasoning. These authors acknowledge the ET presence as authentic and affirm that this presence has been here since biblical times, but they state emphatically that the presence is demonic in origin and intent. Mr. Larson describes the experience of many contactees, the experience of UFO beings giving contactees messages, messages which are consistent with the so-called New Age Movement, revealing a divine inner nature to human beings. Because this teaching is in direct conflict with his interpretation of the Bible, as Mr. Larson explains, he concludes that "extraterrestrials" are demonic beings, part of the delusions prophesied for the end of the age.[63] Mr. Missler and Mr. Eastman entitle a chapter of their book, "Can a Christian be Abducted?"

Their answer is "no," that if one has accepted a personal relationship with Christ, that person will be protected from alien abduction.

My friend and colleague, the Rev. Dr Barry Downing, is a retired Presbyterian minister in Endwell, NY. Dr. Downing has been researching the biblical implications of UFOs and the Bible for the past 30 years. His book, *The Bible and Flying Saucers*, was re-released in 1998 (first published in 1968). Dr. Downing's contends that the angels of God pilot the flying saucers found in scripture. He has incorporated the UFO paradigm into his Christian worldview and theology and finds that it fits quite comfortably. He does not preach a "UFO theology" from his pulpit, and he has yet to be tried for heresy by his denomination. Though I respect his contributions greatly, I do differ with my colleague on this matter. Dr. Downing contends that ETs in the Bible are the angels of God. Space people as wholly benevolent beings (angels) is the position adopted by Dr. Downing. In his view, these beings are here (and most likely have been here for quite some time) to assist us in the fight between good and evil.

I, however, have difficulty justifying the killing of the firstborn male children of Egypt just to prove a point; I do not see that as the action of a loving God, or the action of an angel of God. I do not live in a philosophical world of absolutes; at times the line between what is absolutely good or absolutely evil is gray and blurred. But still, I wrestle with this story. Suggesting that angels killed children is highly problematic for me. In my opinion, it is simply too early in the game to make blanket statements as to whether all UFO occupants in the Bible are really the angels of "God." I do, however, honor Dr. Downing as a pioneer in this field and believe that his work makes tremendous contributions.

It is this writer's opinion that Dr. Downing is clearly the most sophisticated UFO theologian in the country today. He likes to distinguish his own theory from that of Von Daniken and Dione. Dr. Downing says that while he agrees with Von Daniken that the biblical religion was started by beings from another world, he disagrees with Von Daniken's premise that these beings were "God." Rather, Dr. Downing believes that Von Daniken misidentified the ETs as the one God of the universe. Like Von Daniken and Dione, Dr. Downing has made the religion of the Bible more palatable for those with 21st Century scientific tastes. He argues that the Bible cannot be read the same way once an individual is open to the possibility of a UFO influence in Judeo-Christian scripture.

Although many believers in flying saucers maintain that the inhabitants are friendly, this is not the view shared by everyone. There are two opposing premises with regard to aliens: one depicts the aliens as angelic beings interested only in the welfare of humanity and the other looks on aliens as dangerous and terrifying astral entities who are violent and hostile. As with many things in life, perhaps the answer lies somewhere in-between. I propose that the view that there are both benign and malicious super-beings at large in the cosmos engaged in an eternal fight between good and evil is amenable to both philosophical and religious thought.

This worldview can also be harmonized with Christian theology, where the battle between the good and the bad angels represents the universal struggle between the divine and the demonic, a battle that has both divine and earthly significance. The good angels can be said to be the angels sent by God to help humankind, and the evil or demonic ones are here to draw us away from God.

SALVATION

The mission of UFOs is frequently described as one of redemption. Contactees and UFO literature describes several common themes contained in the messages received; among the more common themes are the cure of diseases, the deliverance from the destructive forces of atomic power, and the transportation to a new planet where there will be complete security, wealth, and cooperation. Because of the potential for nuclear war and humanity's proclivity for violence, humanity certainly needs redemption.

In UFO based religions, just as in traditional Judeo-Christian theology, salvation or redemption is conceived as coming from the outside. In other words, while the cooperation of human beings is necessary if the planet and the people are to be saved, the intervention of superior intelligences from other planets is considered essential. More simply put, in UFO-based theology, salvation can be seen as an intervention from space beings that will lead the human race to its next stage of development.

SCIENCE AND RELIGION

Anyone with the requisite historical and psychological knowledge knows that circular symbols have played an important role in every age... they were known as whose center is everywhere and the circumference is nowhere... therefore UFOs could easily be conceived as "gods."
Carl Jung, Flying Saucers:
A Myth of Things Seen in the Skies

Flying saucers also provide contemporary science with an alternative view to that offered by traditional religion and science. Because of the current interest in our culture in the UFO phenomenon, about which science and religion have little to say, people are turning to other sources for information. Many of the answers that religion and science give to some of the questions of life—such as those regarding the origins of the human race—remain somewhat ambiguous, if not contradictory. In a society where religion and science are in conflict, a conflict that creates mainly tensions and contradictions, ufology presents a worldview that brings together religion and science in an apparently harmonious union.

This approach is similar to the Christian fundamentalist insistence that science cannot contradict belief, and further, that beliefs can, in fact, be proven by direct empirical evidence that no honest question can reject. The originality of the worldview that comes with the belief in UFOs is evident when one compares it to the views of the universe that are available in religious creeds and scientific literature. Religion, particularly in the Judeo-Christian tradition, has offered little scope for speculation into the nature of the universe as seen through the eyes of modern astronomical discoveries and scientific achievements. In other words, religious views of the universe are utterly earth-bound. Religious worldviews give human beings a central and significant role in creation; however, they fail to include any theories about the possible existence and theological implications of other intelligent life on other planets. From a literal interpretation of the Bible, one could reach the conclusion that

Earth is located at the very center of the universe and that it is the only place inhabited by intelligent beings, beings who represent the pinnacle of creation. It is therefore not surprising that Christian fundamentalists find it hard to believe that we are being visited by other intelligences from outer space.

One major difficulty with the traditional religious worldview is that it cannot be easily harmonized with modern astronomical knowledge. Original theories about the evolution of human life and its relationship to extraterrestrial intelligence provide a boarder basis for theological reflection. They seek to establish a religious worldview or perspective that places the earth and its inhabitants in a more realistic perspective. By doing so, they establish different theological assumptions about the creation of the world and of the human race, and the involvement of God in the complex process of evolution. In short, the religious problem is that our modern naturalistic system of beliefs makes the Bible appear to be an outdated book of superstition. Dr. Downing laments: "Unless Christian doctrines can be recast into the concepts compatible with modern thought, religious faith will be dismissed. UFOs may be our last hope. If flying saucers do not exist, then much theology will probably continue on the present course which leads down the road to the death of God."[64]

Science on the other hand has all but reduced humankind to an advanced, evolved sample of the animal species. Science will no longer let us believe in angels or miracles, or in the Ascension of Jesus.[65] It does not allow any cosmic significance to being human, nor does it assign any special destiny for human beings, whose chances for survival for a long period of time may not be too promising. The human race remains completely earthbound in its origin and development and can be easily accounted for without recourse to supernatural explanations or extraterrestrial invasions. Because hard physical evidence of flying saucers is allegedly unavailable, scientific theories about the origin and evolution of the human species do not include alien involvement. Speculations or hypothesis about the extraterrestrial origin and/or development of the human race are determined to be unrealistic and far-fetched.

In the UFO paradigm however, unlike the modern scientific or religious worldviews, the origin of humankind is traced, not to the direct, supernatural act of creation by a supreme God, but through physical, natural descent from mighty creatures from other parts of the universe. Unlike the Judeo-Christian view of the universe, this worldview deconstructs the notion of a personal God who intervenes in history. However, this paradigm may take two separate forms. On the one hand, it could adopt a pantheistic view of nature, which sees God not as a person, distinct and separate from the material world, but rather as a spiritual reality in which all of life participates. On the other hand, it could develop a separate worldview, which maintains that the existence and visitations of superior aliens from space are devoid of any supernatural content and can be subjected to the same objective and physically verifiable principles of modern science.

Retired theologian, Ted Peters, professor of Systematic Theology at Pacific Lutheran Seminary, had this to say regarding a UFO theology: ". . . but if we adopt a UFO theology, will all the distinctively religious questions be finally resolved? I suggest that a UFO theology has kicked up a lot of dust, but when the dust settles, we will see that is has simply pushed some questions about the transcendent reality back another step."[66] Obviously Dr. Peters does not buy into the concept of a UFO theology. He added:

> Paul Tillich, the famous Protestant theologian, said that when a five-year old child asks, where did the sky come from? He or she is asking a religious question. It is religious because it questions the source of all reality, the ground of being. This basic question about the ultimate ground of all being is finally, whether the asker knows it or not, the question of ultimate concern. In the past more sophisticated people than our five-year old have asked about the first cause or source of all things... Someone or something originally set things in motion. Aristotle and St. Thomas called it God.[67]

Yet the evidence strongly points to the fact that beings with higher intelligences and supernatural powers from other worlds at certain times in human history have been born on this planet we call earth. Their mission? Who can say for sure? Some have sought to bring about a higher understanding of spirituality for humankind, which we can all agree, is no simple task. Perhaps some of these beings have not had this as their mission. There is extremely powerful evidence that there was extraterrestrial involvement in the life of Jesus, as well as the Old Testament prophets. If this is true (and I believe that it is), we then have to ask, what is the meaning of the enormous number of UFO sightings and contacts in the world today? Biblical scholar and author G. Cope Schelhorn expresses it best when he writes:

What we have been taught in the past our research will discover is often inaccurate and will ultimately fail us. We need clear eyes and an open, agile mind to navigate waters that have most likely been navigated long ago, but for which maps have long been moldering in place, passed by, ignored or misunderstood by the very travelers who need them most.[68]

UFOS AND THE KORAN

"Receiving a visit from outer space seems
almost as comfortable as having a God.
Yet we shouldn't rejoice too soon.
Perhaps we will get the visitors we deserve."
Jacques Vallee

"We all know that UFOs are real.
All we need to ask is where they come from."
Captain Edgar. D. Mitchell Apollo 14 Astronaut, 1971

"Nothing belongs any longer to the realm of the gods
or the supernatural. The individual who lives in the
technical milieu knows very well that there is nothing
spiritual anywhere. But man cannot live without the
sacred. He, therefore, transfers his sense of the sacred
to the very thing that has destroyed its former object: to
technology itself."
Jacques Ellar

As I noted earlier, it seems that UFOs and their occupants can be found in the stories of the world's three monotheistic religions: Judaism, Christianity, and Islam. Let us turn our examination to the Koran. Admittedly, there has not been a great deal written specifically about UFOs in the Koran, but there is some information which may be useful for our purpose, that of confirming the existence of UFOs in the Islamic religion.

The history of religious doctrine is a balancing act between seeing life as it is and life as it could or should be. In the creation of religious doctrine, the past is deemed sacred and viewed as holding inherent wisdom, knowledge, or transcendence. The stories are searched for relevance to life in the present and thought to give meaning to life in the present. Buddhists see The Buddha as the example which leads to Nirvana; Jesus is the example Christians use to live the committed life. These personalities point the way in establishing what it means to be human.

Muslims understand this; the Koran, their Book or sacred scripture, gives them a mission. That mission is to create a just and merciful society in which all are treated with dignity and respect. The political well-being of the Muslim community is a matter of crucial importance. From whence came this focus on justice and mercy to one's neighbor?

Arabia is the world's largest peninsula. Connected from Israel to the African nation of Egypt, it runs through Syria and Turkey. The religion of the region prior to Mohammed was what we today would label a naturalistic religion. That is to say that everything had a spirit, be it a tree, river, rocks, etc. and a spirit was attached to each. The revelations of The Prophet were to radically change Arabia's religious landscape. Mecca was the religious center of the region at the time; a stone or meteorite had fallen from heaven to earth and is still lodged there to this day. The area where the stone fell is called the Kaaba, and each year Muslim pilgrims make the "haaj" or journey to visit this holy shrine. Mohammed was born in the city of Mecca circa 570 C.E. and died in 632 C. E. It appears the name Mohammed derives from the Arabic root *Hamada*, meaning "to praise."[69]

The Koran is divided into 114 Suras or chapters and is roughly the size of the Christian New Testament. [70] For those unfamiliar with the

Koran, biblical figures such as Miriam (Jesus' mother to whom we refer as "Mary"), Moses (known as Musa), and Jesus appear in the book. Jesus appears in 93 verses scattered in 15 Suras. There are also appearances by the angel Gabriel who visits Mohammed while he is in meditation in a cave and commands Mohammed to recite the Koran as it is dictated to him. Recall from the Christian Scriptures that Gabriel was name of the angel who visited Elizabeth, the mother of John The Baptist in Luke chapter 1:19. Also note that Gabriel was the messenger or angel that visited Mary to inform her that she will become the mother of Jesus, Luke chapter 1:26.

According to the Koran, when Gabriel appeared to Mohammed, he had been meditating in a cave on Mount Hira, about 9 miles north of Mecca. Mohammed had gone without food or drink for days when he saw a figure moving toward him, a figure more beautiful than any man he had ever seen.[71]

"Iqra! Recite! Commanded the angel Gabriel." Mohammed refused, but Gabriel was persistent. Again Mohammed was told to recite. Gabriel commanded:

> Reicite in the name of your lord who created —From and embryo created the human. Recite your lord is all giving. Who taught by the pen, Taught the human what he did not know before. The human being is a tyrant, he thinks his possessions make him secure. To your lord is the return of everything.[72]

Mohammed obeyed. This was the first of the revelations delivered to the prophet Mohammed over the next 20 years from which the religion of Islam was born. Initially Mohammed only confided in a few about his revelations and his encounters with the heavenly messenger. The message of social reform given to Mohammed did not win many converts among the warring tribal lords, and attempts were made on Mohammed's life. It was not until the death of The Prophet that the first hardcopy of the Koran was compiled. The word *Koran* (or *Qu'ran* as it is sometimes spelled) means "utterances." The first official compilation of the Koran was made in about 650, twenty years after Muhammad's death, and achieved canonical status.[73] To begin to understand Islam, we must also realize that Muhammad's life was a struggle and that the word, *jihad,* does not mean "holy war," it means to struggle. His struggle was to bring peace to a war torn region where old ways of thinking would no longer suffice. He did this by surrendering to the will of Allah; the religion founded upon the revelations he received is known as *Islam*. The word *islam* means to surrender.

LORD OF THE WORLDS

All throughout the Koran we discover that Allah (God) describes himself with the words, *"Rab-ul-Alameen."* Translated the appellation means, *Lord of the Worlds.*[74] This phrase is used time and again in different chapters of the book:

> And the unbelievers would almost trip thee (Mohammed) up with their eyes when they hear the message; and they say, surely his is possessed! But it (The Quran) is nothing less than a message to all the worlds. (AL –Quran, 68. 51-52)

> Verily, this is the revelation from the Lord of the Worlds. (Al-Quran, 26:192).

> This is no less that a message top (all) the Worlds. (Al Quran, 38.87).

> Soon we shall settle your affairs O'both ye Worlds. (Al-Quran, 55:31).

That Allah identifies himself as Lord of the Worlds is a strong statement because it presupposes more than one world.

Islam recognizes the existence of three separate species of beings. The first are the angels, sometimes referred to as *Malaik,* known as beings of light. There are, of course, human beings. Lastly, there are beings known as *Jinns.*

The *Jinns* are extremely fascinating to me; I have suggested that the so-called angels in the Christian and Jewish scriptures may in fact be ETs. But in Islam, we find an all-together separate category for these beings. I should also note that in New Age thought, ETs and angels are considered two different categories of beings as well.

The literal meaning of the word, *Jinn,* is to conceal one's presence or to hide from observation.[75] There is an entire chapter of the Koran named after these beings; it is written that their presence seen in the skies over Mecca when the verses of the Koran were being revealed to Mohammed.

> Say; It has been revealed to me that a company of Jinns listened to the Koran. They said, "We have really heard a wonderful recital!" (Al-Quran, 46:29).

They are also able to travel through space as is noted:

> And we (Jinns) know that we can not escape Allah on earth, nor can we escape him through flight.

Just like his Jewish counterparts Elijah and Ezekiel, Mohammed was also taken aboard a space craft by a group of *Jinns*. In the first encounter, Mohammed is missing for a full day, and his followers search for him. He is found the next day walking down a hill. When asked about his whereabouts, he explains that the *Jinns* had come to him seeking knowledge. The Prophet traveled with them and was later dropped on a hill top upon his return. Mohammed then showed his companions the mark left by the burning engines of the spacecraft.

> ... He (The Holy Prophet) said, "There came to me an invitation on behalf of the Jinn and I went along with him and recited to them the Qu'ran." He then went along with us and showed us their traces and traces of their fires.[76]

There are many more stories such as this in the Koran. It is my hope that your interest has been peeked enough to research for yourself. It is beyond the scope of this chapter to give an exhaustive account of UFOs in the Koran.

The theories contained within this book are by no means a definitive guide of events; they are simply my theories and nothing more. I wholeheartedly welcome the discussions and debate which I hope will arise from my presentation of these theories. My hope is that people will begin to ponder these things in their hearts and perhaps come to the same or similar conclusions that I have. Extraterrestrial life has been involved with human beings since the beginning of time as we know it.

I believe that these beings have been visiting us since the beginning of human origins and that our ancient ancestors mistook them for gods and built temples in order to worship and emulate them. We are not alone! Consequently, it is by studying our past that we can perhaps begin to understand our present and quite possibly our future. One thing is for certain—We have visitors!

As we have come to the end of this exploration, I will close with the insights of Dr. Robert Jastrow, an internationally known astronomer and the author of *God And The Astronomers*:

> Strange developments are going on in ufology. They are fascinating partly because of their theological implications, and partly because of the peculiar reaction of scientists. . . The scientist has scaled the mountains of ignorance; he is about to conquer the highest peak; as he pulls himself over the final rock, he is greeted by a band of theologians who have been sitting there for centuries.[77]

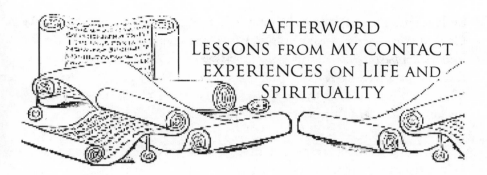

AFTERWORD
LESSONS FROM MY CONTACT EXPERIENCES ON LIFE AND SPIRITUALITY

I must admit that even before my contact experiences I was undergoing quite a significant change regarding my inner life about how the Universe worked and my place in it. For those who are uncomfortable with the word, *spirituality*, I happily use the term, *inner life*, and for those who are uncomfortable with the word, *God*, I suggest you substitute whatever word seems comfortable for you. Perhaps the word, *Life* would suffice instead of the word *God*. . Whatever language you feel comfortable with, please substitute as you see fit. Words can sometimes get in the way when attempting to talk about what is merely beyond words, yet words are all we have. For in reality, the finite can never fully comprehend the infinite. Words are merely symbols for symbols. My concern is simply that I do not want readers to miss the forest for the trees, as the old adage goes.

As a clergy person by calling and profession, my passion lies in what and how human beings experience the divine encounter, whether this experience entail the more mundane interactions of our day to day living, or the mystical, awe filled encounter with which we may label as the *numinous,* or the *mysterium tremendum.* When I began to really delve into the material around the Ancient Astronaut theory and its connection to religion, I have to admit that I was more interested in the contact experiences of our ancestors and the changes that may or may not have occurred in their lives, than I was with propulsion systems and how these spacecraft flew. In short, the "nuts and bolts," of the encounters from a strictly technological point of view bored me.

After and during my encounters, my consciousness shifted to a more global perspective, if you will. More specifically, I began to think about, and to feel, and to take very seriously, that this beautiful blue planet that we live on, was in and of itself a living entity and that we are all inextricably connected. This perspective that I now began to have, that the earth is a living entity, is usually referred to as, "The Gaia Principle." What we do to the Earth we were actually doing to ourselves, and the notion of human beings and nature as being separate from one another started to dissolve.

Now, first of all let me state that for those brothers and sisters who are living in poverty and heartache and merely just trying to survive every day, this principle or theory may not mean anything significant to them right now. Survival was and still is the key for many. Many people are struggling to find and to maintain a job and trying to put food on the table to feed their families. I understand that. As a man of color living many years of my life in an urban environment, I thought that all this talk about saving the oceans and the whales; thinking about our planet, and attempting to understand and protect our ecosystem, was simply something that privileged European Americans, having much too much time on their hands in the first place, was nothing more than a joke. My attitude was that if we could not learn as citizens of the United States, to get over the racism and classism in this country, we would eventually destroy ourselves, and what would it matter about the earth? Humanity would destroy itself and the earth certainly did not need us to survive.

I later came to realize that of course, yes, that it true. The earth does not need us to survive. In the words of Martin Luther King, Jr., "we must learn to live together as brothers and sisters or perish together as fools." Yet the two ideas are not mutually exclusive. We can and very much need to get rid of racism, militarism, sexism, and all of this other, "isms" that we come up with as human beings to keep separate from each other, AND, we are called to be good stewards to this planet which is our home. This earth truly is our Mother and we have been really treating her pretty shabbily for quite some time.

However, this gospel of, *Oneness,* is one of the most important lessons I have learned from my contact experiences from extraterrestrial intelligences. I have come to know that what we call "God," is really an Energy, a Spirit if you like the word; a Source of all Consciousness if you will, and that we are a part of this consciousness. We can tap into this consciousness, if we are willing to, by just being still, through meditation and prayer. You can't heal being by doing. We are called to be human beings, not human doings. This Energy, this Consciousness, this Intelligence, This Infinite Mind, moves through us, in us, and as us. It is all there is. There is no where we can go where this Source is not present. Nowhere.

Period.

Our ancestors mistook our ET visitors as gods because of their technology. We too have made technology at this present time in our planet's history, a god. It is a god of magic. Many people believe that no matter the challenge or problem, technology will save us in the end. This is not to say that technology is wrong. It's just that we have become slaves to it. Most people are so busy now with all of the gadgets that are being advertised now, there is simply anywhere one can go and not be contacted—pun intended. But seriously folks, Smart phones, think pads, tablets, texting, tweeting, emailing, skyping, you name it, we do it. How do we turn off and unplug? Do we even want to?

Now, to be sure, we have been told that many of our ET visitors are much more spiritually advanced than we are, as well as being supremely more intelligent as well. The lesson here is that we need both; we need the insight of both head and heart to be completely human, to be whole. To recognize the connectedness of our planet and the universe is the first step in becoming mature spiritually, or in cultivating an inner life. It is the first step in accepting the diversity of our cosmos. We are barely able to accept the diversity in our neighborhood much less the planet. I am not only speaking of diversity in race or ethnicity. Diversity is so much more than just race. There is diversity in our social economic status, geography, religion, race and ethnicity, sexuality, plurality of thought, and generational diversity, just to name a few. Mature people see beyond these labels, to accept others just as they are. acknowledging what is in their hearts, and ours. A mature species does not use its technology to split the atom and to make war on others. I also came to really understand that we all have a mission that we come to this planet to fulfill. Of course we can choose not to fulfill it and much of our younger years may be used in just trying to figure out what that mission is. Whatever one decides or comes to regarding their mission here, (if they decide to accept it) is that a good part of the mission is to learn to love and to forgive, oneself as well as others. It has often been said that life is a school house here on planet earth and that we go from one set of lessons to another set of lessons throughout our lives here. This does not mean that the lessons are easy. To learn to love, to forgive, to let go, to come to grips with the fact that life is impermanence or constant change, is no easy task.

I've also learned to really appreciate the metaphysical view of life. That there are universal laws that one must follow to live a good life, a life of honesty and transparency. We really do reap what we sow. In the East they call it Karma, in the West we call it Cause and Effect. Our National Security Agencies call it *blowback*. That is to say that when our policies in other countries come back to haunt us or blow up in our faces, we label it blowback. This is why all religions or forms of spirituality concern themselves with how we treat our neighbors. What goes around does eventually come back around. The Universe is intelligent and infinitely wise.

Oh, by the way, THOUGHTS ARE THINGS!!!! We are co-creators in this life and the way we think influences our perceptions of the world and then they manifest. In other words, if you think that life is $#@^%&*?!, and then you die, that is just the what life will mirror back to you. This too is Universal Law at work. We attract to ourselves what we are. If you think you can achieve a certain goal, or if you think you cannot achieve a certain goal, you are right on both counts.

Another lesson that I have learned is that life is not linear and that there are definite cycles to our lives, much like the four seasons we experience, depending on where one resides on the planet. To be sure I was aware of this intellectually, but I now realize that if I am doing the work I need to be doing to become the person I think I am and want to be, it may seem that I am getting the same lessons over and over again, and at times I am, but hopefully, I will be a different person the next time the event comes along. In other words I will handle a situation differently if I have matured and learned the lesson that Life, God, Fate, Destiny, (call it what we will) has to offer. This is an exciting concept for me personally, because for me, nothing is more frustrating than my not having gotten the lesson initially, but when it's the fifth time it had come around and I am just not getting it.

I have also learned that all the answers that I need to have are inside of me. Why? I'm glad you asked. Because this All That Is Consciousness is inside of me. I must admit that I forget this from time to time. In fact, there was a period of time during my initial contacts, when I was not taking full responsibility of my life on some level. A part of me wanted the ET Visitors to take care of the details of my life, and they refused to do it. They had been on some level the catalyst and facilitators for my growth in consciousness and awareness; I may have gotten guidance and direction, but the responsibility of my life was just that---My responsibility! It also reminded me that I am not special because of these contacts, that I still needed to get up in the morning, brush my teeth, and get to work.

I was also shown that I have lived many lives previously through my visions and dreams, and that the gifts and talents that I bring to this life are the gifts and talents that I had developed in other lives. The baggage and growing edges I bring to this life I have also carried over from other lives as well. Aging is necessary. Maturing is optional.

Last but not least is that a reminder is needed for our planet. We need to be reminded that there are as many paths to God as there are people who walk those paths. There have been many Saints, Prophets, and Avatars, who have been sent to our planet to raise human spiritual consciousness down through the centuries. Because of the nature of human oral and written history, it is difficult to say whether or not all of them by E T intelligences, yet one thing is certain. The message of oneness can be traced throughout humanities religious quests, it's just that we don't live it out very well as a collective. Perhaps that will change. It is my sincere hope and prayer that it will. We are so much more than we think we are. We are so much more powerful than we think we are. These have been the lessons and the good news from my contact experiences. We are truly not just citizens of our particular nation states. There is no room for a nationalistic mindset as we enter the second decade of the 21st century. Old wine is not placed into new wineskins. We are cosmic citizens. We are gods and children of the Most High (Psalm 82:6)

Isn't that a lesson worth learning?

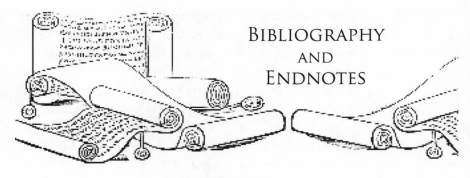

BIBLIOGRAPHY AND ENDNOTES

TEXTS

The Bible: NRSV (New Revised Standard Version), NKJV (New King James Version), the Peshitta (Aramaic Text), and NASB (New American Standard Bible)

Blumrich, Josef F, *The Spaceships Of Ezekiel*. New York: Bantam Books, 1974.

Bramley, William, *The Gods Of Eden*. New York: Avon Books, 1990

Brown, Courtney, *Cosmic Voyage*. New York: Penguin Books, 1996.

Cogswell, John M., "Opening Remarks to the Sitchin Day Lecture," in *Of Heaven and Earth,* ed. Zecharia Sitchin. California: The Book Tree.

Dailey, Timothy, *The Millennial Deception*. Michigan: Baker Books House Co., 1995.

Dione, R. L., *Is God Supernatural? The 4.000 Year Misunderstanding*. New York: Bantam Books, 1976.

Downing, Barry H., *The Bible And Flying Saucers*. New York: Marlowe and Co., 1998.

Drake, Raymond, *Gods and Spacemen in the Ancient East*. New York: Signet Books, 1973.

Eastman, Mark and Chuck Missler, *Alien Encounters: The Secret Behind the UFO Phenomenon*. Idaho: Koninia House Publishing, 1997.

Fowler, Raymond E., *The Andreasson Affair Phase 2*. Oregon: Wild Flower Press, 1982

Fowler, Raymond E., *The Watchers II*. Oregon: WildFlower Press, 1995.

Good, Timothy, *Above Top Secret: The World-Wide UFO Cover-up*. New York: William Quill & Company, 1988.

Greer, Steven, *Extraterrestrial Contact: The Evidence and the Implications*. North Carolina: Granite Publishing, 1999.

Horn, David Arthur, *Humanity's Extraterrestrial Origins*. California: A&L Horn Publishing, 1994.

Jones, Ann Madden, *The Yahweh Encounters: Bible Astronauts, Ark Radiations, and Temple Electronics*. North Carolina: The Sandbird Publishing Co., 1995.

Jung, Carl (Translation by R.F.C. Hull), *Flying Saucers: A Modern Myth of Things Seen in the Skies*. New York: MFJ Books, 1978.

King, George and Richard Lawrence, *Contact With The Gods From Space*. California: The Aetherius Society, 1996.

Lawson, Bob, *Straight Answers on the New Age*. Tennessee: Thomas Nelson Publishers, 1989.

Lawrence, Richard, translation, *The Book Of Enoch*. California: Wizards Bookshelf, 1983.

Mack, John, *Passport to the Cosmos*. New York: Crown Publishers, 1999.

Moore, Charles, "The Orthodox Connection," in *Of Heaven and Earth*, ed. Zecharia Sitchin. California: The Book Tree, 1996.

Oxtoby, William G., ed., *World Religions: Eastern Traditions*. Canada: Oxford University Press, 1996.

Papagiamis, Michael D., "The Search for Extraterrestrial Intelligence and the Possibility of Its Presence on Earth," in *Alien Discussions: Proceedings Of The Abduction Study Conference Held at MIT*, eds. Andrea Pritchard, John Mack et al. Massachusetts: North Cambridge Press, 1994.

Peters, Ted, *UFOs, God's Chariots: Flying Saucers in Politics, Science, and Religion*. Georgia: John Knox Press, 1997.

Red Star, Nancy, *Star Ancestors*. Vermont: Destiny Books, 2000.

Roper Poll, September 2002, for SciFi Channel. Roper Number C205-008232.

Salibla, John, "Religious Dimension of UFO Phenomena," in *The Gods Have Landed: New Religions from Other Worlds*, ed. James R. Lewis. New York: University of New York Press, 1993.

Schellhorn, Cope G., *Extraterrestrials In Biblical Prophecy*. Wisconsin: Horus House Press, 1990.

Sitchin, Zecharia, *The Twelfth Planet*. New York: Avon Books, 1990.

Thompson, Richard L., *Alien Identities: Ancient Insights into Modern Day UFO Phenomena*. California: Govardhan Hill Publishing, 1993.

Von Daniken, Erich, *Chariots of the Gods*. New York: Bantam Books, 1976.

Whitson, William, ed., *The Works of Josephus*. Massachusetts: Hendrickson Publishers, 1987.

PERIODICALS

Berger, Brian, "Exclusive: NASA Researchers Claim Evidence of Present Life on Mars," *Space.com*, February 16, 2005.

Fox, Cynthia, "The Search for Extraterrestrial Life," *Life Magazine*. March 2000.

Howe, Lela, "Astronomy vs. Astrology," *Dell Horoscope Magazine*, May 1996.

Marin, Rich, *Newsweek Magazine*, July 8, 1996.

McKay, David, *Science Magazine*, August 1996.

Sitchin, Zecharia, "Are We Alone?" *UFO Magazine*, February/March 1995.

Szymborska, Wislawa, "The Nobel Lecture: I Don"t Know," *The New Republic*, December 30, 1996.

United Press International, *The Sun Bulletin*, Binghamton, New York. June 21, 1969.

Walker, Marcus, "Ancient Astronauts And Strange Creatures," *Alien Encounters Magazine*, Summer 1996.

ENDNOTES

[1]Professor John Mack, author of the books, *Abduction* and *Passport To The Cosmos,* states that the Contact or Abduction phenomenon challenges the sacred barrier we have created between the visible and invisible worlds. It challenges the fundamental view of the western mind. . . In this culture there may be a small group of scientific, governmental, religious, and corporate elite that determine the prevailing bounds of reality.

[2]I prefer the words "experiencer" or "contactee" as opposed to the words "abducted" or "abduction." I do not feel that I was abducted, and I certainly was not harmed in any way by my visitors. This is not to

deny others their reality or experience. This is simply my opinion and my feelings regarding what happened to me. In my opinion, the terms "abducted" or "abduction" imply a violence or victimization, which I certainly did not feel or experience. Further, one will find that I will use the terms "Visitor," "ET," or "Extraterrestrial." I use the term "ET" or "Extraterrestrial" for the obvious reasons. I use the term "Visitor" because for me that is what they are. "Alien" seems so xenophobic and "other" that the term does not resonate with me. It bothers me that those in the dominant culture will label other human beings who come to this country as "illegal *aliens*". Here ends the sermon for today.

[3]Reiki is a Tibetan healing modality rediscovered by a Japanese Christian named Dr. Usui in the 19th century. Reki was taught in the Mystery Schools of Sumer, Egypt, Babylon, Rome, and other civilizations. The Reiki practitioner channels energy or "ki" into the human energy system by the laying on of hands. The word Reiki means Universal Energy, which we are all breathing in right now.

[4]Roper Poll prepared for the SciFi Channel, September 2002, for use in the Emmy-winning mini-series *Taken*. Roper Number: C205-008232. The margin of error is +/-3%.

[5]Marin, Rich, *Newsweek Magazine*, July 8, 1996.

[6]The show aired on November 25, 1996 at 8 pm EST.

[7]On Wednesday, August 7, 1996, the front page headlines of both *The New York Times* and *The New York Post* featured articles about the "Martian Discovery." The original article was published in the August 1996 issue of *Science Magazine* by Dr. David McKay.

[8]Berger, Brian, "Exclusive: NASA Researchers Claim Evidence of Present Life on Mars," *Space.com*. February 16, 2005.

[9]I appeared in all three of these documentaries; two include my personal experiences and one includes a part of this exploration about *Alien Scriptures*.

[10]Fox, Cynthia. "The Search for Extraterrestrial Life," *Life Magazine*, (March 2000), 48. The *Life* Poll consists of a survey of 1,564 adults, age 18 or older, conducted January 12-13, 2000. The margin of error is +/- 2.5%.

[11] Thompson, Richard, *Alien Identities: Ancient Insights into Modern UFO Phenomena* (San Diego: Govardhan Publishing, 1993), 41.

[12] Good, Timothy, *Above Top Secret: The Worldwide UFO Cover-up* (New York: Quill William Morrow Publishing, 1988), 253.

[13] Greer, Stephen M., *Extraterrestrial Contact: The Evidence and Implications* (Virginia: Crossing Points, Inc. Publications, 1999), 131.

[14] Ibid, 131.

[15] Ibid, 131.

[16] Ibid, 190.

[17] Ibid, 163. The quote by Mr. Davenport can also be found in *USA Today*, in an article on June 18, 1997, written by Richard Price. Emphasis is in the original.

[18] Ibid, 255.

[19] Good, 267.

[20] Ibid, 277.

[21] Ibid, 268.

[22] United Press International, *The Sun Bulletin*, Binghamton, New York, June 21, 1969, 1.

[23] Pagangiamis, Michael D., "The Search for Extraterrestrial Intelligence and the Possibility of its Presence on Earth," *Alien Discussions: Proceedings from the Abduction Study Conference*, held at MIT. Editors, Abdrea Pritchard, John Mack et al (Massachusetts: North Cambridge Press, 1994), 410.

[24] Walker, Marcus, "Ancient Astronauts and Strange Creatures," *Alien Encounters Magazine* (Summer 1996), 66-67.

[25] Ibid, 67.

[26] Paganagiamis, *Alien Discussions*, 408.

[27] Ibid, 408.

[28] King, George, *Contact with the Gods from Space* (California: The Atherius Society, 1996), 17.

[29] Ibid, 35.

[30] Howe, Leslie, "Astronomy vs. Astrology," *Dell Horoscope Magazine* (May 1996), 67.

[31] Walker, 68.

[32]Horn, Arthur, PhD, *Humanity's Extraterrestrial Origins: ET Influences on Humankind's Biological and Cultural Evolution* (California: A&L Publishing, 1994), 87.

[33]Bramley, William, *The Gods of Eden* (New York: Avon Books, 1990), 187.

[34]King, George and Richard Lawrence, *Contacts with the Gods from Space: Pathway to the New Millennium* (California: The Atherius Society, 1996), 42.

[35]Ibid, 43.

[36]Thompson, Richard, *Alien Identities: Ancient Insights into Modern UFO Phenomena* (California: Govardhill Publishing, 1993), 213.

[37]Ibid, 259.

[38]Red Star, Nancy, *Star Ancestors* (Vermont: Destiny Books, 2000), xiii.

[39]Von Daniken, Eric, *Chariots of the Gods* (New York: Bantam Books, 1976), 5.

[40]Dione, R. L., *Is God Supernatural? The 4,000 Year Misunderstanding* (New York: Bantam Books, 1976), 7.

[41]Sitchin, Zecharia, "Are We Alone?" *UFO Magazine* (Feb/March 1995), 11.

[42]Cogswell, John M., "Opening Remarks to Sitchin Studies Day," In *Of Heaven and Earth*, editor Zecharia Sitchin (California: The Book Tree, 1996), 5.

[43]Moore, Father Charles Louis, "The Orthodox Connection." In *Of Heaven and Earth,* editor Zecharia Sitchin (California: The Book Tree, 1996), 31.

[44]Ibid.

[45]Schelhorn, G. Cope, *Extraterrestrials in Biblical Prophesy* (Wisconsin: Horus House Press, 1989), 3.

[46]Downing, Barry H., *The Bible and Flying Saucers* (New York: Marlowe & Company, 1997), 79.

[47]Jones, Ann Madden, *The Yahweh Encounters: Bible Astronauts, Ark Radiations, and Temple Electronics* (North Carolina: The Sandbird Publishing Group, 1995), 1.

[48]Blumrich, Josef, *The Spaceships of Ezekiel* (New York: Bantam Books, 1974), 3.

[49]Brown, Courtney, *Cosmic Voyage: A Scientific Discovery of Extraterrestrials Visiting Earth* (New York: The Penguin Group, 1996), 34. According to much of the UFO literature, the so-called "Blondes" or "Swedes" are the benevolent ET entities, while the so-called "Grays" and others are evil. The "Blondes" are often referred to as handsome or with perfect facial features, from a traditional Western cultural perspective. In my mind, these perceived differences have triggered an automatic stereotyping to occur within the dominant culture regarding the intentions of these beings. If we were a society in which racism was absent, I would not raise the issue here.

[50]Fowler, Raymond, *The Watchers II* (Oregon: WildFlower Press, 1995), 355-356.

[51]Ibid, 356.

[52]The birth of Jesus, John the Baptist, and Samson, among others, were initiated by an angel.

[53]Timothy Dailey has a PhD from the Moody Bible Institute and is a conservative Bible literalist, as are Bob Larson, Chuck Missler, and Mark Eastman. However, unlike most clergy or theologians, these men do acknowledge the existence of ET life. These authors are very much interested in the apocalyptic and eschatological aspects of the UFO phenomenon.

[54]Oxtoby, William G., Editor, *World Religions: Eastern Traditions* (Canada: Oxford University Press, 1996), 223.

[55]Ibid, 223. Buddha's mother is married but under a vow of celibacy, whereas Mary is said to be an unwed virgin. Both infants are born outside their family homes—Jesus in a stable and Buddha in a grove. A bright light announces both births, and sages forecast their future greatness. Also, angels appear in the sky to announce the births, to shepherds in the case of Jesus and to a mediating sage in the case of Buddha.

[56]Bramley, William, *The Gods of Eden* (New York: Avon Books, 1990), 123.

[57]James, Joses, Simon, and Judas, all brothers of Jesus, were most likely conceived in this way. Jesus is said to have had sisters as well, and so it does appear that Mary did experience her sexuality as a woman. See Matthew 13:55-56.

[58]Whitson, William (translator), *The Works of Josephus* (Massachusetts: Hendrickson Publishers, 1987), 480. Emphasis mine.

[59]Downing, 126.

[60]Drake, W. Raymond, *God and Spacemen in the Ancient East* (New York: Signet Books, 1968), 43.

[61]Szymborska, Wislawa, "The Nobel Lecture: I Don't Know," *The New Republic* (December 30, 1996), 26.

[62]Salibla, John, "Religious Dimensions of UFO Phenomena," in *The Gods Have Landed: New Religions from Other Worlds*, ed. James A. Lewis (New York: State University of New York, 1995), 34.

[63]Larson, Bob, *Straight Answers on the New Age*, (Nasheville: Thomas Nelson Publishers, 1989), 289.

[64]Ibid, 13.

[65]Downing, 12.

[66]Peters, Ted., *UFOs: God's Chariots in Politics, Science, and Religion* (Georgia: John Knox Press, 1977), 116.

[67]Ibid, 117.

[68]Scelhorn, xii.

[69]Inturralde, Robert, *The UFO Phenomenon and The Birth of The Jewish, Christian, and Muslim Religions.(Bloomington, Indiana: AuthorHouse, 2009) p. 229*

[70]Ibid. p. 230.

[71]Ibid. p. 231.

[72]Armstrong, Karen, *Muhammed,* (New York, New York, Atlas Books: HarperCollins, 2006), p. 45-46.

[73]Ibid. p. 16.

[74]Abdul Aziz Khan, *UFO's In The Quran, (New York, New York; Strategic Book Publishing, 2008) p.117*

[75]Ibid. p.119.

[76]Ibid. p. 124-125.

[77]Fowler, Raymond E., *The Andreason Affair Phase II* (Oregon: WildFlower Press, 1982), 213.

ABOUT THE AUTHOR

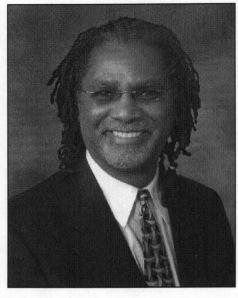

Rev. Michael J. Carter is originally from Baltimore, Maryland. He moved to New York City in 1980 and lived there for 25 years, working as a professional actor before moving to Asheville with his family. Michael is an ordained Interfaith minister and received his BA Degree in Letters from the College of New Rochelle where he graduated cum laude. He received his Masters In Divinity Degree from Union Theological Seminary in New York City (class of 2000). While serving various Unitarian Universalist Congregations in New York, Michael was trained as an anti-racism trainer and has been recognized by President Clinton for his efforts. Michael was also a weekly columnist for the Asheville Citizen Times. Rev. Carter now serves as the minister for Unitarian Universalist Congregation of The Swananoa Valley, in the beautiful mountains of Western North Carolina.

Rev. Carter has written articles on UFOs and Religion for such publications as UFO Magazine, Alien Encounters (A British Publication),The MUFON UFO Journal, Contact Forum, The S.P.A.C.E. Newsletter (Support Program for Abductees Contact Encounters) a UFO support group in New York City. He has spoken at UFO Conferences such as the 2nd Philadelphia, Need To Know Conference, The Annual Long Island UFO Conference with Budd Hopkins, as well as appearing on radio and TV appearances across the nation. Rev. Carter has also appeared on Japanese television discussing the Bible and UFOs.

A long-time UFO experiencer, he lectures extensively on the topic of religion and UFOs. He has appeared on the Sci-Fi Channel's Steven Spielberg's production of *Abduction Diaries, The Real 4400*, and is a frequent guest on The History Channel's production of *Ancient Aliens*.

To learn more about Rev. Carter's other works and television appearances visit http://www.MichaelJSCarter.com

Made in the USA
San Bernardino, CA
29 December 2019